The Authors

Maralene and Miles Wesner are multi-talented teachers and prolific writers. They have published more than 150 Audio-Visual Education aids, and pioneered new reading methods with their Phonics in a Nutshell (1965).

They have written articles, and mission studies for Southern Baptist periodicals. They were in the original group of writers to develop WMU's Big "A" Club material.

They've published several books with Broadman Press: *A Fresh Look at the Gospel* (1983); *You Are What You Choose* (1984); and *How To Be a Saint When You Feel Like a Sinner* (1986) and self-published 30 books by Diversity Press.

They are noted for their no-nonsense style, their clear illustrations, and their willingness to face controversial issues. From the dual perspectives of both academic and religious professions, they seek to be a bridge between the spiritual and the intellectual worlds.

They hold Masters Degrees (MEd) from Oklahoma University plus work toward a Doctorate. Miles also attended Southwestern Baptist Theological Seminary, and served as a high school counselor. He has been the bi-vocational pastor of a small rural church for more than 50 years.

Both Maralene and Miles taught in public school and collages and served as educational consultants. Maralene taught Psychology and Speech for Southeastern Oklahoma State University for 32 years. She was chosen Oklahoma Teacher of the Year in 1975.

They have planned, led tours, and done research in all of the 50 states, Canada, Mexico, Europe, Egypt, Japan, and the Holy Land. In 1985, they were among a small group of Americans who were invited by Dr. Joseph P. Kennedy of the US/China Education Foundation and Bishop Ting, leader of the Three Self Movement, to participate in the First Symposium on the Church in Nanjing, China.

Now, they use their lifetime of varied experiences to write insightful sermons, essays, and books.

Titles by Maralene & Miles Wesner
published by Nurturing Faith

Sermons for Special Days

Life More Abundant

Do You Really Know Jesus?

If Jesus Were Here Today

101 Sparks of Inspiration

When God Can't Answer

Think
(OR ELSE!)

Maralene & Miles Wesner

Contents

Preface

It's okay to have different opinions, but it's not okay to twist and shade and change facts to fit our own desires.

In the past most of us received our information from a few well-documented reference books and from our own honest and caring mentors. Now, true and false, good and bad, right and wrong statements flow around us constantly. They come from TV, radio, movies, music, Facebook, Twitter, and innumerable people with malicious intent, trying to brainwash us for their own purposes.

Never have our thinking skills been so tested or so important. Our democracy depends upon our ability to discriminate between reality and propaganda. Even our faith depends upon our ability to separate truth from superstition. Our very existence depends upon our willingness to base our lives upon logical principles rather than unrealistic delusions.

Christianity must be a thinking religion. These short articles and devotionals are not intended to be debate briefs or argument starters. They simply represent one person's viewpoint on relevant issues. We hope these insights will either validate your current observations or stimulate you to develop your own authentic observations from a different perspective. In times like these, we really must "think, or else." In this case "or else" means we'll lose our freedoms, and possibly our very lives, if we don't think.

Part 1:

Thinking About Personal Problems

Aimlessness

Many of us are indecisive, uncertain, and inconsistent. The reason we don't get what we want is because we don't really know what we want.

One study found that only three percent of people have written goals. Seven percent have a fuzzy idea, and ninety percent have no idea at all. Follow-up surveys reveal that the three percent with written goals achieve more than the rest put together. Paul said, "I press on toward the goal" (Phil 3:14).

Some of us confuse wishes with goals. We say, "I wish I were a better parent"; "I wish I could go back to college"; "I wish I could lose some weight." But a wish by itself does nothing. Then people confuse activity with accomplishment. A scientist put a caterpillar on the rim of a flowerpot. Inside, he placed the worm's favorite food. The caterpillar began crawling around the rim, smelling the food, and trying to reach it. It crawled around for seven days until it died of starvation. Working harder by itself is not enough.

Sometimes we have contradictory goals. We need to be with our children, and we need to finish a work project. Since our time is limited, we can't do both, so we have dissonance. Many people want new careers, new relationships, new houses, new recreations without considering the cost in time and effort that it will take to get and maintain those wants. Instead, we must pick the thing we want most. If we plan, perform, and persevere, we'll be able to achieve it.

Jesus had a purpose from childhood. At the age of twelve he said, "Did you not know that I must be in my Father's house?" (Luke 2:49).

Apathy

Once, Jacob awoke from sleep and made a significant observation: "Surely the LORD is in this place—and I did not know it!" (Gen 28:16).

Are we really that unaware and apathetic? Over and over, we hear people say, "I never thought about it!"; "I never noticed!"; "I didn't realize that!"

Thinking requires effort, and most of us avoid that. Most of us run on instinct and habit rather than rational thought. We do what we've always done. We do what authority figures tell us to do. We choose the easiest way rather than the most productive way. We make the quickest response rather than the best response. We are reactive instead of proactive.

Apathetic people simply let life happen. They have no goals, no ambition, and no initiative. A man said, "I took my little boy fishing. He put down his pole and started munching on doughnuts. I began casting and soon had a nice bass.

Then I caught two more. My son complained, 'Dad, how come you're catching all the fish?' I said, 'Well, I guess it's because I keep my hook in the water. You can't catch fish eating doughnuts.'"

It's the same with life. When you see an individual getting compliments, honors, and promotions, it's usually because they've invested time and effort in their job.

Authenticity

In Hans Christian Anderson's story "The Ugly Duckling," a little bird tries desperately to be something he's not. When he finally realizes discovers his true identity, he says, "Being born in a duck yard doesn't matter if you are really hatched from a swan's egg."

Shakespeare said, "To thine own self be true; then it follows as the night the day, thou canst not be false to any man!"

Jesus repeatedly admonished people to be genuine and real. He criticized those who pretended to be something they were not. He condemned hypocrisy, saying, "Beware of false prophets, who come to you in sheep's clothing but inwardly are ravenous wolves" (Matt 7:15).

He also said, "Woe to you, scribes and Pharisees, hypocrites! For you are like whitewashed tombs, which on the outside look beautiful but inside are full of the bones of the dead and of all kinds of uncleanness" (Matt 23:27).

A new Christian said, "I always assumed believers were supposed to act alike. I thought God was recruiting a spiritual trumpet corps with a lot of identical members. If we carefully watched the players around us, we'd know just how to hold our trumpets. Finally, I learned we were not supposed to sound alike. Instead, God gives each of us our own individual sound." Some people live as if they are piccolos trying to play in the tuba section.

Each person is unique. Jesus didn't choose twelve clones for disciples. He chose twelve different individuals. Peter and John and Thomas and James each had distinctive traits and temperaments and interests.

When it comes to authenticity, we can learn from nature. Each animal is different, and that's okay. The beaver doesn't frustrate itself trying to fly like an eagle or climb like a mountain goat or develop the strength of a bear. Instead, a beaver's instinct keeps saying, "Be a beaver. Just be a beaver!" That's being authentic!

Autonomy

Someone said, "We're born to win but conditioned to lose." This negative conditioning starts early. A shy little boy was proud of a picture he had painted. But when some kids laughed at it, he was hurt and embarrassed. Years later, a college professor discovered he had a real talent for art. Unfortunately, painting caused him to have panic attacks. After therapy he became an award-winning artist. Nevertheless, one wrong opinion had almost destroyed his potential.

Our self-image is practically set by the age of six or seven. That's why most of us go through life never really knowing who we are and never really understanding why we act the way we do. We need to become autonomous and confident. Paul said, "Each one of us will be held accountable" (Rom 14:12).

As children we need a nurturing person to affirm us. We need caretakers who validate our feelings. If parts of us are accepted (e.g., our smiles) and other parts are rejected (e.g., our angers, griefs, and fears), then these rejected parts get split off. They will continue to grow outside of our consciousness and cause unexplained rage, depression, or anxiety.

An old man said, "I grew up being told, 'Big boys don't cry! Good boys don't yell! It's sissy to be afraid!' I couldn't even be very happy because there were starving children in Africa. The only legitimate emotion in my family was guilt." If you can't be sad, mad, or glad, your true self shuts down, and a false self is created.

God wants us to be real and honest.

Blots, Blessings, and Blanks

Hitler was a blot on the landscape of life. He was almost totally negative and destructive. He hated and hurt and killed.

Schweitzer was a blessing to the hosts of humanity. He was almost totally positive and constructive. He loved and helped and healed.

Most of us, however, are neither complete blots nor complete blessings. We're somewhere in between. We tend to be rather neutral. Instead of being blots or blessings, too many of us tend to be blanks. We may not leave heel marks, but neither do we leave footprints. We may not subtract from life, but neither do we add to it. We may not tear down, but neither do we build up. When we die, life will go on as if we had never lived. What a shame!

Let's not be a blot or a blank. Let's be a blessing! Let's leave the world a little better than we found it.

Paul said, "Whenever we have an opportunity, let us work for the good of all" (Gal 6:10).

Blue Mondays

People who suffer from depression are at risk. Some people take their own lives. Many others cause accidents, get sick, or abuse alcohol and drugs.

Unfortunately, these individuals don't wear warning labels. Instead, they look like everyone else. In fact, they may even smile and declare that they feel fine.

Research discovers various causes of severe depression: the weather, the season, the lack of light, chronic pain, losses, stress, guilt, etc. Genetic temperament is a contributing factor. Sometimes there is a family history of depression. Hormones, biological chemicals, and medication can also affect a person's emotional outlook.

Profiles of depression-prone individuals are interesting. They are often highly intelligent professionals who feel driven to reach high ideals and accomplish worthy goals. In fact, there is often a fine line between the manic depressive and the outstanding leader.

Some depression attacks can be traced to a specific event. Others seem to come "out of the blue."

People in the throes of depression may be delusional. Everything becomes bigger than life. Little things get blown out of proportion. All events are related to them, and every evil in the world becomes their burden.

Depression can actually be unexpressed anger turned inward. Some people punish themselves for their real or fancied sins and weaknesses.

Depression can also be used to punish others. Suicide attempts may be calls for help, or they may be efforts to make family and friends feel guilty.

Everyone has an occasional "blue Monday," but if you're depressed for a long period of time or if you have radical mood changes, get help!

The psalmist said, "Why are you cast down, O my soul?... Hope in God" (Ps 43:5).

Building Our Houses

Being a Christian is a serious matter. Jesus said, "Everyone who hears these words of mine and does not act on them will be like a foolish man who built his house on sand. The rain fell, and the floods came, and the winds blew and beat against that house, and it fell" (Matt 7:26–27).

An elderly carpenter told his employer he was planning to retire. The contractor was sorry to see his good worker go and asked if he would build one more house as a personal favor. The carpenter agreed, but his heart was not in his work, and he used inferior materials and allowed shoddy workmanship.

When he finished, the contractor came to inspect the house. Instead, he handed the key to the carpenter. "This is your house," he said. "This is my gift to you for your years of service."

What a shock! What a shame! If he had only known he was building his own house, he would have done it all so differently. Now he had to live in what he had built. That's everybody's story.

If we base our lives on immoral values and develop our character in a haphazard way, then we'll have to live in what we have built.

Burdens or Blessings?

A naturalist watched an ant struggling down the sidewalk with a long straw in its jaws. As the little insect approached a wide crack in the concrete, the observer thought, "Now he's doomed. He'll fall into that hole and be buried alive"

Instead, that ant was positive and creative. When he reached the crack, he laid his awkward load across the space and crawled over to the other side. Then he picked up his burden and continued his journey.

The ant turned his liability into an asset. He saw his problem as an opportunity. His burden became his bridge. Do you have any liabilities you could turn into assets? Do you have any problems you could use as opportunities? Do you have any burdens that could become bridges?

No matter what mistakes you've made, they can be used for good. No matter what failures you've had, they can become learning experiences. No matter what sins you've committed, they can be forgiven. Our burdens of the past can become our bridges to the future.

That's what Paul meant when he said, "We know that all things work together for good for those who love God" (Rom 8:28).

Busyness

Being busy makes us feel useful and important. In fact, a person who is not overcommitted is sometimes considered to be lazy and irresponsible. But commitments can be like plants in a garden. If there are more than the soil can support, then none will thrive.

To be successful we must set reasonable limits. Decide how many responsibilities you can handle, and don't over promise. Choose which organizations and projects to support. Realize that if you try to juggle too many balls, they will all fall down.

People who are too busy become impatient and ineffective and eventually burn out. Instead, do what interests you. Do what you are good at. Do what is most productive.

Rushing around, trying to squeeze in more stuff than you can handle causes you to do everything less well and makes everything less enjoyable. Don't be too busy!

Jesus paced himself. The scripture says, "[Jesus] would slip away to deserted places and pray" (Luke 5:16).

The Cat and the White Cord

Our Siamese cat is deathly afraid of white cords. We discovered this phobia when we put a heating pad in her basket under some towels. When she dug down to the bottom of her nest and found the white cord, she abandoned that basket forever. No amount of coaxing would get her near it.

We got her at the age of six weeks, so evidently she'd had a traumatic experience with a white cord when she was very young. Maybe she bit into one and it shocked her. At any rate, her defense mechanism now says, "Avoid white cords!"

To solve the problem, we painted the cord black and changed baskets. Everything was fine.

Many of our own phobias lead to similar behavior. Often we don't even know the causes of our fears. We feel we must avoid certain people, places, or things in order to survive. Some of these defense mechanisms may still be valid, but others need to be eliminated.

To find your "white cords," ask, "What hurt me in childhood? What defense mechanisms did I develop? What fears, habits, and perversions did I acquire? What did I have to do to get love? To get approval? To avoid punishment?"

Then tell yourself, "I don't have to use those mechanisms anymore! Things are different now."

Also realize that your mate and other associates have their own survival mechanisms. Realize that they, too, are probably totally unaware of them.

In fact, most of us are "flying blind." We're on automatic pilot. We're simply playing out the patterns of our past.

It's important for us to understand why we have certain "hot spots" and "trigger points" and "white cords." We must understand these irrational fears and urges before we can overcome them.

The psalmist said, "The LORD...delivered me from all my fears" (Ps 34:4).

Changing the Past

Changing the past is an impossible task. Since we can't go back in time and undo our mistakes, many of us spend the rest of our lives wallowing in guilt. We become obsessed with why we did or didn't do something.

Of course, hindsight is 20/20, but remember that as you were living through those times, things weren't quite that clear. Don't judge yourself too harshly. Our less-than-perfect actions can be forgiven and even redeemed. Since we're products of our past, these old mistakes and tragedies can be used in our growth process. Paul said, "We know that all things work together for good for those who love God" (Rom 8:28).

We are who we are today because of our personal experiences. If we changed our backgrounds, we wouldn't be "us." The trials we've passed through have shaped us. The poor decisions we've made have taught us. There is no other way to mature or gain strength. We may look back and wish things had been different, but that's futile.

In the grand scheme of things, there are no isolated incidents. All things merge and become part of the flow. Even the bad can work together with the whole for good. What we are now is the result of what has gone before.

Someone said "If Abraham Lincoln were living today, he'd probably be on welfare." His deprivations and hardships may have actually increased his integrity and wisdom.

Therefore, don't regret. Don't punish yourself. Don't project your disappointments and frustrations onto those around you. Instead, say, "I am here as I am because of my past experiences. If things had been different, I wouldn't be me!"

Channel, Don't Change!

"He had a charismatic personality, excellent communication skills, and unusual leadership abilities." Surprisingly, this description is equally applicable to either Hitler or Jesus Christ.

It's obvious that the same traits can be used for destructive or constructive purposes. That's why it's hard to pinpoint a particular quality and say, "That's bad" or "That's good." A qualifying value depends upon its use. For example, a child who is impatient, demanding, and bossy may become a hated dictator or a successful executive. A child who is careless with money and rather unconcerned about his possessions may become a worthless spendthrift or a generous philanthropist. A child who tells tall tales and seeks center stage may become an obnoxious egotist or a spellbinding performer.

You see, traits are neutral. In fact, negatives can actually be perverted or misused positives. Therefore, trying to fix people or alter their natural tendencies is nonproductive . People can't change their basic natural traits, but they can channel them in ways that will achieve positive results.

Peter said, "Whoever serves must do so with the strength that God supplies" (1 Pet 4:11).

Crawl Before You Walk

Individuals, groups, and entire civilizations mature in stages. Each living entity moves from birth into infancy, childhood, adolescence, adulthood, and old age. You can't skip a stage. You can't leap from infancy to adolescence or from adolescence to old age. In short, you gotta crawl before you can walk!

Many well-meaning people don't understand this. Some benefactors think you can turn a baby into an adult by giving him a steak and a credit card. It can't be done!

Some missionaries think you can yank a convert from Moses's "Sinai mentality" to Paul's "Calvary mentality" in one evangelistic service. It can't be done!

Some politicians think you can impose a full-blown twenty-first-century democracy on a twelfth-century monarchy in one election. It can't be done!

There are no shortcuts in the maturing process. There are no shortcuts from the point of primitive superstitions to the point of scientific technology. There are no shortcuts on the road from autocracy to autonomy. The passage can be encouraged, facilitated, and accelerated by education and encouragement, but each state must be experienced and lived through. You gotta crawl before you can walk!

Even Jesus grew. The scripture says, "Jesus increased in wisdom and in years and in divine and human favor" (Luke 2:52).

Deadly Videos

Carrying a grudge about an injury is the ultimate evil. It gives more pain than the original event. Every time you remember being cheated or criticized or betrayed, you hurt. Every time you think about the person who did the wrong, you hurt. After a while, your memory becomes a deadly videotape playing reruns in your soul.

That's stupid! You are punishing yourself for other people's sins. The only way to heal is to forgive. When you "let it go," you actually change the memory. When you stop the deadly "video," you set yourself free.

Carrying guilt about something you have done to someone else is the flip side of this evil. It, too, gives more pain than the original event. Every time you remember cheating or criticizing or betraying someone else, you hurt. Every time you think about the person you wronged, you hurt.

Again, your memory becomes a deadly "video" playing reruns in your soul. That, too, is stupid! Punishing yourself over and over for your past sins is useless. Instead, admit them, confess them, and atone for them if possible. Then let them go!

This, too, changes the memory. When you stop the deadly reruns, you set yourself free!

Paul said, "One thing I have laid hold of: forgetting what lies behind and straining forward to what lies ahead" (Phil 3:13).

Deferred Gratification

The desire for instant gratification is wrecking our economy. Today, people are consumed by desires to buy things they don't need with money they don't have.

We are impulsive. We don't consider the consequences of our actions. We don't connect causes and effects. This is especially true if the effects are not immediately evident. We say, "I'll do what I want to now and worry about the consequences later."

We're impatient. We can't wait. We take shortcuts. We skip steps. We want rewards without effort. We buy now and pay later.

In fact, a deferred gratification pattern is not even considered a value in our materialistic society. Yet, according to research, a deferred gratification pattern is the one criterion that determines success.

When a Vietnamese couple arrived in America, they were flat broke and spoke no English. A cousin who owned a bakery in a mall let them live in a back room and work in the shop. He offered to sell them the bakery for a reasonable sum.

With a small weekly income, the man and his wife lived in the back room, took sponge baths in the mall's restrooms, and ate the leftover bakery goods. In two years they had saved enough for the down payment.

The man explained, "If we got an apartment, we'd have to pay the rent. Then we'd have to buy furniture. We'd have to buy a car. Then we'd have to buy gasoline and insurance. I knew if we got that apartment, we'd never save enough."

There's even more to this true story. After they made the down payment, they still owed a sizable amount, so the couple decided to keep living in that back room for one more year. They saved every nickel of profit, paid off the note, and owned the business free and clear. Then they got their first apartment.

The scriptures support such frugality. Solomon said, "The plans of the diligent lead surely to abundance, but everyone who is hasty comes only to want" (Prov 21:5).

Doing What Comes Naturally

"Doing what comes naturally" may be the old song's advice, but are we really sure what's natural and what's not? A youngster who has always eaten whale blubber thinks that's natural. A kid raised on hamburgers and French fries thinks that's natural. A child who's been abused thinks that's natural.

You see, whatever we've done all our lives seems natural to us. Whatever we've been taught to believe seems natural to us. Whatever condition we've experienced over a period of time seems natural to us. Whatever treatment we've received in our youth seems natural to us. In fact, it's hard to convince a squirrel that's been in a box for two years that the forest is his natural habitat. It's hard to teach a child who's been neglected and abused that love is his "natural right."

How, then, can we help a person let go of a familiar negative past that feels natural and reach out to a positive but unfamiliar future that feels unnatural? First, we must explain how the status quo is destructive and demonstrate a better way. Next, old patterns must be changed; old habits must be broken. As we realize that what feels right may only be what's familiar and that what feels wrong may only be what's unfamiliar, we'll be able to adjust and accept a new and better life.

As Isaiah said about the child, we must be able to "refuse the evil and choose the good" (Isa 7:15).

Doing Your Own Thing

Some of us find it hard to focus and "do our own thing" because everybody else in the world is pressuring us to do their thing. It seems everyone has their hand out for our money. Everyone is hyping a project that requires our participation. Each group, organization, and institution wants us to help them promote their agenda. If we don't immediately abandon our own and begin to support theirs, they become resentful and assume we're unconcerned.

This is a fallacious attitude. Since life is limited, there's a finite amount of time and money available. None of us can do it all. None of us can join every organization, even every beneficial organization. None of us can finance every institution, even every great institution.

Different charities serve different needs, and different movements focus on different issues. In the final analysis each of us must find and follow our own path.

We may join with others, or we may go alone, but associates should not take it as a personal rejection when we say, "I appreciate you, and I wish you well, but I must do this!"

In fact, if our agendas are both valid, they'll eventually verify and validate each other. My road and your road will meet in the end if they're both on target. It takes my agenda, your agenda, and everybody else's agenda to achieve ultimate success. We shouldn't view differing agendas as antagonistic. I shouldn't spend my time trying to get you to do my thing. Instead, I should do my thing. You shouldn't spend your time trying to get me to do your thing. Instead, you should do your thing. If everyone did that, then all the things would get done.

Perhaps we engage in enlistment rather than achievement because we aren't sure about our own agendas. Perhaps we get upset when others concentrate on their paths rather than ours because we're insecure and need the reinforcement of like-minded partners.

These outlooks aren't productive. Just because you are interested in different aspects of life, just because you are seeking answers to different questions, just because you are bent upon finding solutions to different problems doesn't make mine less important. If our purpose is worthwhile, then we'll discover that everyone working on their own personal agenda is best!

Peter said, "Serve one another with whatever gift each of you has received" (1 Pet 4:10).

False Self-Images

Many of us develop false self-images because, from birth, we see ourselves in the mirrors of our family and friends and teachers. Too often, those mirrors reflect distorted images.

As children we evaluate all the looks, remarks, and actions of those around us and decide, "This Is Who I Am." We base our self-image on what we've been told, whether it's accurate or not. This determines what we can and cannot do. If someone says, "You'll never amount to anything," we believe it.

Furthermore, from then on, we'll look for evidence to support that opinion and filter out any information that contradicts that opinion.

Mary, a middle child, was always described as "cute and sweet." She was never encouraged to excel. Her parents thought her brother was a genius, and since her little sister was pretty, they pushed her into music and dance. Mary remained "cute and sweet" even though she was as intelligent as her brother and actually more musically talented than her sister. Today, as a mediocre college student who's "cute and sweet," she's still being faithful to her assigned image.

As children we never question the validity of these evaluations. Our identity and personal worth are established early in life. If the setting is too low, we'll live down to that set point, and the wrong setting will become a self-fulfilling prophecy. Like thermostats, we change the circumstances to make them fit our setting, whether it's high or low.

Jesus knew who he was, and he had a high level of self-esteem. When criticized once, Jesus answered, "Is it not written in your law, 'I said, you are gods'? If those to whom the word of God came were called 'gods'—and the scripture cannot be annulled—can you say that the one whom the Father has sanctified and sent into the world is blaspheming because I said, 'I am God's Son'?" (John 10:34–36).

Jesus had a true self-image.

"Fear" Itself

When Franklin Roosevelt said, "The only thing we have to fear is fear itself," few people understood what he meant. It sounds senseless and contradictory! Nevertheless, it expresses a profound and dangerous truth.

Fear nullifies our sense of independence. It overrides our reasoning ability. It reduces us to a weak and vulnerable state. It causes us to do illogical and destructive things. It makes us susceptible to bullying and bondage.

Immoral tyrants know this and use it They do this to keep us in subjugation. Every dictator from Caesar to Hitler has been a fearmonger. A frightened populace is an easily manipulated populace. The fear of loss, the fear of ridicule, the fear of the unknown are all good tools in a controller's hands. Don't fall for these schemes! Don't succumb to these tactics!

Legitimate fears can protect us, but manufactured fear can be our greatest enemy. The scripture tells us that God doesn't want us to be afraid; instead, he gave us "a spirit of power and of love and of self-discipline" (2 Tim 1:7).

The Bible also says, "Perfect love casts out fear" (1 John 4:18).

Feel and Deal

Amid stress and violence, depression and suicide, divorce and burnout, we want a magic formula that will fix things. Politicians promise government programs. Evangelists promise religious miracles. Advertisers promise materialistic fulfillment.

Unfortunately, none of these will help unless they are linked to personal responsibility. The answers lie within us! We must learn how to "feel and deal."

Whether our problems reveal themselves in domestic abuse, drug addiction, alcoholism, or simply restlessness and misery, we can change our lives dramatically by learning to feel and deal.

From childhood we're taught to hide our true emotions: We must not be afraid. We must not be sad. We must not be angry. Now, of course, we do feel all these things, but we deny them, suppress them, and relabel them. Little boys can't be "sissies," so sadness and fear are acted out as aggression. Little girls can't be assertive, so desires for independence and decisiveness are acted out as "manipulation." By the time we are adults, most of us have lost touch with our true feelings.

To feel we must become aware of our true emotions and desires. We must admit them honestly. We must understand where they come from. We must express them in "I" language. To name something is to control it. As long as these vague feelings remain unacknowledged and unidentified in the basement of our subconscious, they will ruin our lives. Analyzing them, confronting them, and labeling them will enable us to handle them.

To deal we must develop coping mechanisms. We must integrate our feelings into our personalities and use them for growth. If the feelings are violent, we can have "time out" signals. We can take walks or exercise. If the feelings are depressing, we can find hobbies or recreational outlets. Above all, we can realize that our emotions are legitimate. Feeling is not a sin! It's acting out these feelings in destructive or inappropriate ways that becomes immoral.

James said, "I by my works will show you faith" (Jas 2:18).

Grandiosity

We must realize that life has limitations. There are only twenty-four hours in a day. A human only lives a finite number of years.

A woman known for her exuberance came into a nursery to discuss a wonderful new garden she was planning. This "blue garden" would be awesome.

She dominated the conversation for an hour about what different flowers in shades of blue would require as to sun and shade and moisture and fertilizer. When she left, someone said, "Man, I can't wait to see that project when she's finished." The owner of the store, who knew her well, laughed and said, "Finished? My dear, that woman's potted geranium died last month because she forgot to water it."

Too many of us are like that. We imagine tremendous achievements that never materialize. We start epic productions and then abandon them. Our magical thinking bypasses common sense. We expect to win the lottery or find the pot of gold. We look for magnanimous bailouts. We indulge in golden fantasies.

Grandiosity includes idealism. Only great ventures interest us. Ordinary tasks are dull and boring. An immoral businessman once told Mark Twain his plans for the future. "Before I die," he boasted, "I'm going to make a pilgrimage to the Holy Land and read the Ten Commandments aloud on the top of Mt Sinai."

"I have a better idea," said Twain. "Why don't you stay right here at home and keep them?"

Grandiosity creates delusions. We underestimate the amount of time, energy, and resources such projects will require.

Grandiosity encourages perfectionism. Everything must be flawless. We lose interest if defects are discovered or if the project doesn't quite live up to our standards. Therefore, many things are started and never finished.

An old proverb says, "He who attempts too much accomplishes little." Solomon says, "Keep sound wisdom and prudence" (Prov 3:21).

The Importance of Self-Concept

Our self-concept determines our morality and our productivity. It's ironic that people with low self-esteem experience very little dissonance when they sin or fail. That's because committing an immoral or unsuccessful act is not at odds with their self-concept. If I believe I'm bad, then doing a bad thing seems reasonable.

On the other hand, people with high self-esteem experience great dissonance when they sin or fail. If I believe I'm good, then doing a bad thing seems wrong.

That's why our self-concept is so important. It influences our conscience and determines our behavior. If I believe I'm kind, then an unkind action causes dissonance. If I believe I'm smart, then an ignorant action causes dissonance. If I believe I'm frugal, then a wasteful action causes dissonance. If I believe I'm successful, then an unsuccessful action causes dissonance.

In order to be happy, we must have consonance. That means our beliefs and our actions must match.

James tells us to avoid being unstable, hesitant, and uncertain about what we feel and think (see Jas 1:8).

I Quit!

We hear, "When at first you don't succeed, try, try again! Never give up! Keep on keeping on! Winners never quit, and quitters never win!"

Persistence is considered a great virtue, and it is! But is there ever a time to quit? Well, Jesus said there was: "If anyone will not welcome you or listen to your words, shake off the dust from your feet as you leave that house or town" (Matt 10:14).

In fact, Jesus quit certain projects. When his ministry in Judea became too dangerous, the scripture says, "Jesus therefore no longer walked about openly among the Jews" (John 11:54).

Of course, realizing you're on a dead-end street and changing directions is quite different from giving up entirely and quitting life.

A certain man decided to drill a well. Neighbors had successfully hit water at relatively shallow depths. This man drilled down fifty feet—no water. He drilled to one hundred feet—no water. He drilled to two hundred feet—still no water.

Finally, he decided to accept his loss, pull out of the hole, and drill in another location. Was that wise? It's hard to tell. Should he have persevered, saying, "I'm going to drill this hole to the bitter end"? Or did he do the right thing when he decided, "This is obviously a dry hole. It's time to cut my losses."

We don't know the answer to that question. But there's always a time to persevere and a time to quit. Unfortunately, knowing which to do in a specific situation is one of life's most difficult decisions.

Justifying Our Mistakes

We often try to justify our mistakes and excuse our failures. One man who had several business deals go bad was convinced it was because of his bald head. Picking out something in our life that we can't change and making it the cause of all our problems limits our future. If we believe fate has dealt us a bad hand, we'll be a loser.

People say, "If only I had married a different woman, things would be better. If only I had chosen a different college, I wouldn't be flunking. If only my parents had done a better job. If only my pastor had not disappointed me. If only my company hadn't transferred me."

Such excuses are useless. They accomplish nothing. We are personally responsible for our lives. We'll never develop responsibility if we justify our mistakes and make scapegoats of our parents, our church, our boss, the stars, or the government when things go wrong. Sometimes people even try to hold God accountable, but James says, "No one, when tempted, should say, 'I am being tempted by God,' for God cannot be tempted by evil and he himself tempts no one. But one is tempted by one's own desire, being lured and enticed by it" (Jas 1:13–14).

Don't justify or excuse your mistakes. Learn from them and correct them!

Learned Helplessness

We're born to be autonomous and confident individuals, but too often we develop learned helplessness—the feeling that nothing we do can make a difference.

Years ago, researchers put dogs in closed cages and gave them electric shocks. At first they tried to jump out, but after a few days they gave up. Later, even when the tops of the cages were removed, these animals still made no effort to escape. They believed they were helpless.

Those with such learned helplessness say, "What's the use? Effort doesn't pay."

Unfortunately, it seems that way at times. Once, an ambitious man worked his way up from bagging groceries to becoming assistant manager. He was a dependable employee who put in long hours. He deserved a promotion and was promised the position of manager. But at the last moment the absentee owner gave the job to his inexperienced nephew. The ambitious man was devastated. He left the grocery business and tried college but flunked out. He lost several jobs and finally lost his family. His attitude had become, "Why try? It's the breaks—not your effort—that matter." He had learned helplessness.

Before you were born, God had a plan and a purpose for your life. He gave you the special abilities and aptitudes that would enable you to accomplish that purpose. Now it's your job to discover who you really are and to do what you are meant to do. That requires autonomy and a willingness to follow God's guidance. The scriptures say, "'I know the plans I have for you,' says the LORD, 'plans for your welfare and not for harm, to give you a future with hope'" (Jer 29:11).

Don't let other people's opinions—or even a few failures—determine your worth or make your choices.

Little Things

It's not always momentous events that make a difference. It's not always bold, dramatic deeds that change the world. More often than not, it's the everyday activities done faithfully that lead to success.

The scripture tells us that one small stone killed Goliath (see 1 Sam 17:49).

Jesus especially emphasized the idea that little things matter. He used one little boy's lunch to feed a multitude (see John 6:9).

He said faith the size of a mustard seed can move mountains (see Luke 17:6).

He stated that simply giving a cup of cold water deserves a reward (see Matt 10:42).

He also praised many unknown heroes. Andrew wasn't a major figure in the scriptures, but he "brought his brother, Peter, to Jesus." Without this one act, we may not have had Peter, who reached over three thousand souls on the day of Pentecost (see John 1:35–42).

Ananias was a humble layman who ministered to Paul in his blindness, led him to the Lord, and baptized him. Without this plain, uneducated man, we may not have had Paul, who wrote half of the New Testament and spread the message of Jesus to the gentile world.

When a sinful woman simply put perfume on Jesus's head, he said, "Wherever this good news is proclaimed in the whole world, what she has done will be told in remembrance of her" (Matt 26:13).

You see, quiet, unseen individuals doing small, ordinary tasks avail much. Little things mean a lot. Don't ever say, "My contribution doesn't matter."

Masks

Most of us wear masks. Now, it's reasonable to adapt to different situations and different people. But if the mask begins to distort our true self, we'll forget who we really are. Each of us is born as a unique individual with special characteristics and abilities. We must remove our masks and analyze our personal traits to discover our natural temperament.

There are four basic personality types with an infinite number of possible blends. Everyone is different. Furthermore, there are no bad or wrong temperaments. The scripture says, "Train children in the right way, and when old, they will not stray" (Prov 22:6).

We can't change our natural temperaments. We must be who we were meant to be. A woman said, "A scary creature with twisted features rang my doorbell on Halloween. I quickly dropped some cookies into his bag, and he hurried away. The next day, my little paper boy said, 'Those sure were good cookies you gave me last night!' I could hardly believe it! This handsome child was behind that ugly mask."

Sometimes it works the other way. An ugly creature wears a beautiful mask. Once, a shopper bought an ornate antique chest with large gold letters on the lid that read, "Treasures." But when she looked inside, she found a lot of rusty junk. The outside and the inside did not match.

People who try to hide their natural temperaments are like that. We may wear masks because we were told as children how we should be. We may try to copy someone else, or we may be influenced by the media or peer pressure, but it won't work.

An old poem says,

> The orchid's not a daisy,
> And the lily's not a rose.
> The plants don't spend time trying
> To be something else that grows.
>
> The bluebird's not a robin,
> Nor the crow a chickadee.
> So sing the song God gave you,
> And be what you're meant to be.

Maturity

Immaturity is rampant. The writer of Hebrews was disgusted when Christians failed to grow. He said, "Though by this time you ought to be teachers, you need someone to teach you…. You need milk, not solid food…. Solid food is for the mature" (Heb 5:12–14).

Being mature means being fully developed. But reaching maturity is a process. We grow in different areas. A great scientist said, "We're technical giants but ethical midgets." The scripture says, "Jesus increased in wisdom and in years and in divine and human favor" (Luke 2:52).

In other words, we grow intellectually, physically, spiritually, and socially. A person may be forty-seven years old chronologically but only four years old emotionally. Once, a woman called a psychologist and said, "I need help. My son has a treehouse, and he wants to live up there all the time."

The doctor laughed. "Oh, that's probably just a phase. He'll get over it!"

"Yeah," answered the mother, "but now he wants his wife and kids to move up there with him."

To be mature we must look, think, feel, and act as an adult. A person who is totally selfish and egocentric; who constantly whines and throws pity parties; who only talks about "me," "my," and "mine" is not mature.

A person who has his wants and needs mixed up, who is never satisfied and is always chasing some new and novel fad is not mature.

A person who has no ability to delay gratification, who will trade away a productive tomorrow in order to have a brief pleasure today is not mature.

Paul said, "When I became an adult, I put an end to childish ways" (1 Cor 13:11).

Immaturity causes most of our personal and social problems.

Mindset

Many of us don't have a mindset; rather, we have our "mind set." We are stubborn. We reject valid information. We have blind spots. We refuse to rethink our beliefs. We don't want to change our behavior. We close down and say, "My mind's made up! Don't confuse me with facts."

Isaiah said, "They do not know, nor do they comprehend; for their eyes are shut, so that they cannot see, and their minds as well, so that they cannot understand" (Isa 44:18).

Some people think they already have the "truth." Since they are absolutely right, they don't need to listen or learn or change or grow. A bucket can sit out in the rain for three days and not have a drop in it—if the lid is sealed tight. That's the way our mind is when it's "set."

Too many of us are like the man who, when he was served Brussel sprouts, said, "No thank you! I've never eaten them because I don't like them!" How did he know? Mindset can be deadly! If a new idea creates dissonance by contradicting something we already believe, we'll ignore it, deny it, or quickly forget it.

Jesus realized the dangers of mindset. He said, "This people's heart has grown dull, and their ears are hard of hearing, and they have shut their eyes, so that they might not look with their eyes, and hear with their ears, and understand with their heart and turn—and I would heal them" (Matt 13:15).

My Toothache

Everyone has problems and pains. One grieving woman went to a wise man and asked for a charm that would protect her from further tragedy. He said, "Yes, I will give you such a charm if you bring me a handful of dirt from a home that has never experienced sorrow."

The woman went from house to house asking, "Have you ever had trouble or grief?"

Over and over, the people sadly nodded their heads. As she went around the country learning about her neighbors, her heartache changed. She stopped being overcome with her own sadness and became sympathetic toward those around her.

It's been said that your own burdens grow lighter as you share others' burdens. We all have burdens, and ours seem to be the worst. We're like the little girl who told her dentist, "I have the worst toothache in the whole wide world."

"Why do you say that?" asked the dentist.

"Because," she replied, "it's my toothache."

Paul also reminds us to be concerned about our neighbor's problems, saying, "Bear one another's burdens" (Gal 6:2).

Of Guilts and Anxieties

Like most things in this world, guilts and anxieties can be either good or bad. Both are essential human motivators. They are good because they discipline us and make us more responsible.

Guilt over past mistakes keeps us from repeating destructive behavior. Criminal psychopaths are those unfortunate individuals who seem unable to feel guilt. They have no empathy and therefore continue to harm others. They never express regret or sorrow over their deeds.

Paul explained it this way, saying, "I rejoice, not because you were grieved but because your grief led to repentance" (2 Cor 7:9).

Sorrow sometimes makes a person change his mind.

Anxiety over future decisions makes us foresee possible negative consequences and plan ahead. "Blithe spirits" are those unfortunate individuals who seem unable to link cause and effect. They are totally impulsive and therefore continue to "leap before they look." They never exercise prudence or caution before making crucial decisions.

Jesus advised us to avoid anxiety about tomorrow. but he also said, "Which of you, intending to build a tower, does not first sit down and estimate the cost, to see whether he has enough to complete it?" (Luke 14:28).

Solomon said, "The wise are cautious and turn away from evil" (Prov 14:16).

Some guilts and anxieties are productive; others are unproductive. Wallowing in remorse without doing anything to rectify our past mistakes is useless. Worrying and fretting without doing anything to prevent future problems is useless.

Therefore, those guilts and anxieties that only make us miserable but do not affect our behavior should be eliminated.

Of Needs and Wants

We need water. We want Coke. What's the difference? Well, water is basic and essential for life, and the desire for water is a biological instinct. Coke, on the other hand, is superficial and nonessential to life, and the desire for Coke is a conditioned habit. We don't always want what we need or need what we want.

We need bread; we want candy. We need exercise; we want entertainment. It's fairly easy to differentiate needs from wants at the physical level, but it's much harder at the emotional and mental levels.

Emotionally, we need love, but we want sexual gratification. Mentally, we need truth, but we want intriguing gossip. Spiritually, we need God, but we want worldly excitement. We need self-worth, but we want fame. We need joy, but we want pleasure. We need fulfillment, but we want money.

You see, our needs and our wants get mixed up, and the lines between them get blurred. Out of ignorance and desperation we pervert our natural needs into unnatural wants. The more difference there is between our needs and our wants, the more immature and unproductive we are. The more similarity there is between our needs and our wants, the more mature and productive we are. In fact, it's only when our needs and our wants have become synonymous that we are whole.

Paul says, "My God will fully satisfy every need of yours" (Phil 4:19).

Of Winners and Losers

"It isn't whether you win or lose; it's how you play the game."

This statement usually means, "I need a 'face-saving device' to rationalize my loss." No one really believes that winning is unimportant. Anyone who claims losing is as much fun as winning is lying.

Even so, there are always winners and losers, and no one likes a sore loser. So what's the answer? Well, there are two ways of reacting to loss.

The first reaction is destructive because it explains away, denies, or excuses the loss and blames the opposition: "I didn't get a fair shake"; "The race was rigged"; "The umpire was biased"; "The opponent cheated"; "It's not my fault. I really won, but the victory was stolen from me." Such responses take away the joy of the winner and teach me nothing.

The second reaction is constructive because it's honest. It says, "I'm sorry"; "I'm angry"; "I'm disappointed"; "I wanted to win, but I didn't."

I must discover the reasons for my loss and learn from them. If the contest was truly rigged, then I must avoid such situations in the future. If I have weaknesses, they must be strengthened. If my methods are flawed, I must correct them.

In any case I must admit my true feelings.

Of course, winning or losing matters. I don't become a good loser by lying and saying, "I don't care." I become a good loser by analyzing my losses and shaping them toward future wins.

Paul was able to handle his disappointment, saying, "I have learned to be content with whatever I have" (Phil 4:11).

Perfectionism: Its Cause and Cure

Perfectionism can be unhealthy and nonproductive. It's unhealthy because it increases physical and mental stress. The perfectionist is hard on himself, and he's hard on his associates.

Many highly successful individuals are driven by perfectionism. They can't forgive themselves for being fallible human beings. They are prime targets for hypertension. The sociological damage is even worse. These perfectionists know deep down that they are less than perfect. Therefore, they tend to be defensive. They constantly point out the flaws in others to reassure themselves.

Judging and criticizing makes perfectionists miserable and unpopular. They need to admit their imperfections. John said, "If we say that we have no sin, we deceive ourselves" (1 John 1:8).

They need to realize that a minister's "respectable sins" are just as bad as a criminal's "despicable sins." James said, "Whoever keeps the whole law but fails in one point has become accountable for all of it" (Jas 2:10).

This scripture shows the vulnerability of the strong and gives hope to the weak. We haven't killed anyone, but have we made critical remarks about anyone? If so, we are guilty. We haven't committed adultery, but have we been selfish and greedy and lazy? If so, we're guilty. We haven't stolen anything, but have we resented an opponent's good fortune? If so, we're guilty.

Even Paul, who wrote much of the New Testament, recognized his imperfection and said, "Not that I have already…reached the goal, but I press on" (Phil 3:12).

When a perfectionist realizes his infinite worth before God, he experiences a great liberation. He sees that it's okay to make mistakes, to fail, to be a human being. It's even okay to be less than perfect.

Persistence

A philosopher said, "Everybody is enthusiastic at certain times. Some have enthusiasm for thirty minutes, others for thirty days. But it's the person who has enthusiasm for thirty years who is successful!"

Jesus believed in persistence. He said, "No one who puts a hand to the plow and looks back is fit for the kingdom of God" (Luke 9:62).

Most of us promise and then forget. We start and then quit. We commit and then fail to follow through. We give up too soon.

There are many reasons for this. Sometimes it's because we're rebellious. We don't want to do what we're told to do. Sometimes it's because we're impulsive. We jump in without thinking. Then, by the time we realize the project is not possible or productive, we've already wasted time, energy, and money.

Sometimes it's because we try to do too many things. We take on too much. Then we either lose interest or become overwhelmed and drop out.

A church in Georgia was built by slaves who worked at night by the light of bonfires. The women brought bricks in their aprons. The phrase on the cornerstone described their dedication: "The man who laid the first brick was the man who laid the last."

Too often, we become discouraged in the middle of a project. But when we're tempted to quit, we must remember this scripture: "Let us not grow weary in doing what is right, for we will reap at harvest time, if we do not give up" (Gal 6:9).

A college student almost dropped out during his last semester. But his grandmother was adamant. "You can't quit," she declared. "I've already bought a congratulations card for your graduation."

Paul could say, "I have finished the race; I have kept the faith" (2 Tim 4:7).

Pitfalls in Life

Jesus said, "The gate is narrow and the road is hard that leads to life, and there are few who find it" (Matt 7:14).

What a tragic reality! So many lives are in shambles. Some have already crashed under the acute pain of divorce, violence, drugs, alcohol, bankruptcy, illness, or death. Many others are slowly crumbling from the chronic miseries of frustration, disappointment, depression, regret, worry, boredom, and uncertainty. Thoreau called these "lives of quiet desperation."

Each of us has only one life, and it's too valuable to waste. Therefore, if the path is narrow, we must find it and stay on it. Unfortunately, inadequate maps, deceptive signboards, false guides, dead-end streets, aggravating roadblocks, and time-wasting detours plague all of us.

Job expressed it this way: "A mortal, born of woman, few of days and full of trouble, comes up like a flower and withers, flees like a shadow and does not last" (Job 14:1).

Fortunately, Jesus can help us avoid those pitfalls. He said, "I came that they may have life and have it abundantly" (John 10:10).

Procrastination

The writer of Hebrews says, "Today, if you hear his voice, do not harden your hearts" (Heb 3:7–8).

A restaurant posted a sign that read, "Free meal tomorrow." Many people returned for the free meal, but the sign didn't change. It never read, "Free meal today." This scheme got more patrons in the diner, but no free meals were ever granted.

A talented painter spoke constantly of creating his masterpiece. When questioned, he'd always say, "Oh, I didn't get around to it today. Maybe tomorrow"; "I didn't really feel like painting today. Maybe tomorrow"; "The light wasn't quite right today. Maybe tomorrow."

When he died, a friend put these words on his tombstone:

> He was going to be all a person could be, tomorrow;
> And no one will be greater or better than he, tomorrow.
> But the fact is, he died and then faded from view,
> and all that was left when his living was through,
> was a mountain of things he intended to do, tomorrow.

We emphasize good intentions rather than solid accomplishments. If we "mean" to do it, we use that as a substitute for actually doing it!

We emphasize verbalization rather than performance. If we say all the right words and express our plans as a promise, we don't feel a need to follow through. We emphasize later rather than now. If we can find any plausible reason to delay a task, we do.

When making an important decision, always ask yourself, "Which will be more important in the future—this achievement or this distraction?"

Jesus said, "We must work…while it is day" (John 9:4).

Selective Perception

We tend to see what we want to see and hear what we want to hear. Jeremiah said, "Hear this, O foolish and senseless people, who have eyes but do not see, who have ears but do not hear" (Jer 5:21).

Most of us ignore certain information. If something is disturbing, we either "don't see" it or quickly forget it. Mark Twain said, "When I read something I don't agree with, I write it down because I know I won't remember it." In fact, all of us have a natural tendency toward selective perception. For instance, what a baby sees and hears early on determines what he will notice later. Researchers have found that if normal kittens are only around vertical lines for the first eight weeks, they will later walk right into horizontal slats. In short, anything that's not stimulated in infancy atrophies.

In primitive times, this was a survival mechanism. Nature assumed the environment of our first few years would remain the same for life. But that's not true in a changing world! For instance, chickens are programmed to notice and avoid black flying objects but not huge steel objects. That's why more are killed by cars than by hawks. Sociologists discovered more New Yorkers are afraid of snakes than of trucks. Yet in Manhattan they are much more likely to be injured by vehicles than copperheads.

Such selective perception does not serve us well today. To be knowledgeable we must understand all areas of life and be objective and realistic. We can't filter out what's unpleasant or disturbing. We can't pick and choose. We can't throw away the parts we don't like. We must not deny facts or distort information to suit ourselves.

Jesus said, "Blessed are your eyes, for they see, and your ears, for they hear" (Matt 13:16).

Self-Discipline

No one enjoys discipline. Nevertheless, discipline is necessary. Furthermore, discipline from parents and authority figures must lead to self-discipline. The lack of discipline leads to inertia. A woman said, "Once I saw a flower seed display in a feed store. As I looked at the wonderful pictures, I got excited and bought five packages. When I got home, I ran out to the garden to begin, but I found a clump of hard ground full of weeds. As I stood beside the miserable little plot, reality set in. I realized this would take a lot of work—pulling weeds, hoeing, tilling. I went inside and laid the seeds on my windowsill. They were still there in December, reminders of a garden that never grew."

The lesson of self-discipline is to live your belief or let that belief go. If you aren't actually involved in getting what you want, you don't really want it. Thoughts, feelings, and actions must match. The head, the heart, and the body must work together. If these three are out of sync, nothing is accomplished. Thoughts plan the process and analyze the consequences. Feelings motivate the interest and the enthusiasm. Actions accomplish the task. The writer of Ecclesiastes said, "Whatever your hand finds to do, do with your might" (Eccl 9:10).

Self-discipline is important!

Self-Image

Each of us has a self-image that affects everything we do. If it's negative and destructive, we live down to it. If it's positive and constructive, we live up to it.

This self-image is the setpoint of our lives. For example, if I see myself as "cool and competent," I'll set up situations that show this side of me and avoid situations that might challenge it. I'll be attracted to people who recognize and validate those traits, and I'll be repelled by people who ignore and discount them.

A self-image is developed early in life by the way we're treated and the way we respond to that treatment. This self-image can be good or bad.

If we see ourselves as failures, we'll actually sabotage our own efforts and lose jobs and businesses.

If we see ourselves as givers, we'll be vulnerable to scam artists and beggars.

If we see ourselves as brains, we'll try to know everything and cover up any lack of knowledge.

If we see ourselves as helpers, we'll get bogged down in good organizations and volunteer work.

Once our self-image is defined, we'll defend it when it's threatened and work day and night to keep it intact. Even if it limits us, we'll protect it as long as it functions reasonably well. It's only when something happens to shatter our self-image that we are willing to reevaluate it. The crisis might be the loss of a career, bankruptcy, a divorce, an illness, the death of a loved one, or an accident. Such things crack our shell and force us to alter our outlook.

What is your self-image? Consider these questions: What compliments please you most? What criticisms anger you most? What weaknesses do you try to hide?

Evaluate your self-image. Is it positive or negative? Realize that self-image is not sacred. It's not set in stone. It was given to you by other people and life experiences, and you have a right to change it if it's not productive!

Paul explains that we can be transformed by the renewing of our minds (see Rom 12:2).

Uncorrected Weaknesses

No one is perfect. Every strength has a potential weakness. That weakness can be the opposite of the strength or even the strength carried to extremes. Some people need approval, attention, and excitement. They will say what they think people want to hear to please them, but then they don't follow through. Their weaknesses may include lack of focus, discipline, or persistence.

Other people are controllers who will even break rules to prove their independence and get their way. Their weaknesses may include impatience and domineering behavior.

Some people just don't fit in. They may become withdrawn and reclusive. When they're hurt, they're vulnerable to depression and guilt. Their weaknesses may include resentment, moodiness, or pessimism.

Then there are people who always seek the easy way. They will agree to almost anything to limit confrontations. They avoid the difficult situation or say, "I forgot." Their weaknesses may include procrastination or indecision.

Even small defects and distracting habits can hinder us. A woman said, "Last spring, my hazelnut tree looked weak and sick. My uncle said, 'You need to cut down these bushes growing around the base of the tree.' I asked, 'How can these little bushes bother the tree?' He replied, 'They are sapping its strength.' I pulled out the bushes, and by the end of the summer, my tree had healthy leaves and a bumper crop of nuts."

Little things can impede our progress and sap our strength. We need to recognize, admit, and avoid our debilitating weaknesses. John said, "If we say that we have no sin, we deceive ourselves, and the truth is not in us" (1 John 1:8).

Unproductive Guilt

President Harry Truman said, "The buck stops here!" For some of us, however, not only our buck but everybody else's bucks seem to stop here! Over the years we take on the problems of the world. We assume responsibility for our relatives and acquaintances. We feel guilty if anyone anywhere fails at anything.

Because we're insecure, we punish ourselves with criticism and condemnation. We push ourselves to be all things to all people. We fragment ourselves to give little pieces of our time and energy to everyone who needs us. Inevitably, we begin to burn out and become resentful. We still serve, but we do it reluctantly and out of a sense of duty. Furthermore, we lose ourselves in the process.

This is an unproductive, futile undertaking. One person can't meet every need and fulfill every desire. No person is omniscient! No person is omnipresent! No person is omnipotent! It's prideful and delusional to think we can hold the world together singlehandedly.

If we're real and honest and open, then we can be God's partners, but we can't be God. Some bucks should stop here, but others must be sent on their way. If the bucks pile up, so does the guilt. Guilt that motivates us when we shirk our responsibility can be productive, but guilt for things beyond our control is a sin!

God freely forgives—and even forgets—all our sins (see Heb 8:12).

Unproductive Life Script

Many of us have unproductive life scripts. We follow these scripts until they become habits. We can't develop our own agenda because we've been trained to obey the demands of authority figures. We're not sure if we want to do certain things or if that's just what our parents or teachers wanted us to do. For instance, a boy who's into athletics may wonder if that's even his interest or if that's his frustrated dad's interest. A girl who's into beauty pageants may wonder if that's her own interest or if that's her disappointed mother's interest.

We choose certain recreational activities because our friends enjoy them. We decide on certain careers because our mentors or media idols influence us. We accept certain volunteer positions because our pastor urges us to. We agree to certain political or civic responsibilities because of public pressure. In short, we are not in charge of our own lives.

A script is a life plan. It's like a drama written for a stage production. We often feel obligated to play our assigned role and do exactly what the script dictates. The son of a successful lawyer assumed he would also become a lawyer. Now, this young man had artistic abilities and really wanted to be an architect, but he felt he would betray something or someone if he did that, so he never even considered this profession. Instead, he went to law school and is dutifully playing a role he did not choose and living out a script he did not write.

God's life script for us is productive. The scripture says, "I know the plans I have for you, says the LORD, plans for your welfare and not for harm, to give you a future with hope" (Jer 29:11).

Wants or Needs

Most of us don't know what we want, but we are quite sure this isn't it. When our basic needs are unfulfilled, we develop a lot of wants.

We need status. To have this we seek more power, more prestige, and more fame. There's never enough, so we have shame and guilt and anger.

God fills our status needs by emphasizing our value. Jesus said, "You are of more value than many sparrows" (Luke 12:7).

We are sons and daughters of the king. God says, "I will be your Father, and you shall be my sons and daughters" (2 Cor 6:18).

We need assurance. To have this we seek more money, more possessions, and more relationships. There's never enough, so we have worry and fear and frustration.

God fills our assurance needs by promising his presence. Jesus said, "I am with you always, to the end of the age" (Matt 28:20).

Solomon said, "One who trusts in the LORD is secure" (Prov 29:25).

We need sensation. To have this we seek more amusement, more pleasure, and more excitement. There's never enough, so we have boredom and apathy and depression.

God fills our sensation needs by giving us purpose. Jesus said, "Make disciples of all the nations…teaching them to obey everything that I have commanded you" (Matt 28:19–20).

He also said, "You will be my witnesses…to the ends of the earth" (Acts 1:8).

These things we think we must have to be happy often become addictions. Then we try to use these addictions to fill our basic legitimate needs. Unfortunately, dealing with addictions makes us even more anxious and frustrated. Let God fill your real needs, and that will take care of your wants.

Who Are You?

Who we are is determined by three things: heredity, environment, and choices. In other words we are born with certain special traits, abilities, and tendencies. Then, during our early childhood, parents and teachers and events influence and affect our development. Finally, as adults we are able to make conscious logical decisions concerning our attitudes and behavior.

It's as if when we buy a car, it comes equipped with certain features—that's heredity. Then the weather and road conditions affect its performance—that's environment. Finally, it's the driver himself who has the greatest influence on how it operates and where it goes—that's choice!

Who are you? A bundle of animalistic instincts? A creature of cultural conditioning? A free, autonomous spiritual being?

This question is easy for Christians to answer. Paul states clearly, "We are children of God" (Rom 8:16).

Part 2:

Thinking About Relationship Issues

Aggravation

A crop of dandelions grew on a young man's lawn. He tried everything to get rid of them. He wrote the Department of Agriculture so many times that they finally lost patience and responded, "Dear Sir, About those dandelions—we suggest you learn to live with them!"

Many things that make us angry must be accepted. Our loved ones and friends may have mannerisms that annoy us, but if we care for these individuals, we may have to learn to live with their foibles.

Some things that make us angry can be used. Jesus tells of one man who channeled his anger productively. When certain guests rudely rejected his invitation, he offered it to others! In a parable he said, "The owner of the house became angry and said to his slave, 'Go out at once into the streets and lanes of the town and bring in the poor, the crippled, the blind, and the lame" (Luke 14:21).

This man could have retaliated against the rude guests who spurned his invitation, or he could have brooded over their rudeness and done nothing. Instead, he adapted his plans and achieved ultimate success.

All of us have anger at times. It's a natural response designed to protect us, but when it's misused, it destroys us, our family, our community, and our world. It causes spouse abuse, child abuse, road rage, and violent murders.

Solomon said, "Those who are hot-tempered stir up strife, but those who are slow to anger calm contention" (Prov 15:18).

Anger

Everyone gets angry. Even Jesus got angry. Paul said, "Be angry but do not sin" (Eph 4:26).

When we do get angry, a calm, reasonable analysis is essential. Such an evaluation should include at least one of these statements:

> My anger is inappropriate. This was my fault.
> My anger is silly. This was an accident.
> My anger is overblown. This was unimportant.
> My anger is misplaced. I am really mad about something else.
> My anger is justified. This was wrong!

If we honestly assess that the anger is justified, then instead of a wild, unproductive reaction, we can let that anger become a positive motivator.

Jesus used his anger to confront those who imposed oppressive rules that hurt people. Once, when a crippled man begged for help, the people demanded that he must not be healed on the Sabbath. The scripture says, "[Jesus] looked around at them with anger; he was grieved at their hardness of hearts" (Mark 3:5). Then he healed the man.

Anger can be a very destructive force or a positive catalyst for change. Use it well!

Being Different Isn't Wrong

Once, a little boy and his grandfather both looked at the same man. One said, "That's my son." The other said, "That's my dad."

Who was right? Should they have disagreed and argued and fought about the factual validity of those statements? Should they have ridiculed and criticized each other? Should they have become hostile and angry because of their differences? Of course not! There's more than one way to express truth. Two opinions can be different without one of them being wrong.

It's only ignorant individuals who must constantly dispute what others say. It's only arrogant individuals who must always defend their positions as the only correct way to think. Intelligent people can allow and even encourage diverse opinions and varied belief systems.

Of course, we should never allow or encourage the dissemination of false information or evil, hurtful speech. But simply having different viewpoints and opinions should not make two people or two groups or two nations destined to become mortal enemies.

Paul said God will be the judge (Rom 14:5–10).

Being Right or Being Kind?

Most of the time, being right on doctrinal and ethical issues is synonymous with being kind. Most of the time, being kind is synonymous with being right. Occasionally, there is a conflicting situation when you can't be both right and kind at the same time. Then what do you do?

Well, Jesus faced this dilemma over and over again. It was right according to Old Testament laws to refrain from activities on the Sabbath, but it was kind to heal hurting people. It was right according to Old Testament laws to avoid all contact with sinful people, but it was kind to touch the prostitutes and eat with the publicans. It was right according to Old Testament laws to condemn and even stone adulterers, but it was kind to forgive them.

In every case where being right and being kind were in conflict, the Lord chose kindness. Unfortunately, Christianity has been weak in this area. Too often, we are judgmental and arrogant and self-righteous. We treat other religions with disdain. We condemn those who differ in beliefs. We denounce those who fail to keep all our rules.

How right are we when our attitudes and actions cause people to become defensive and hostile? How right are we when we force people to choose unbelief and cynicism? How right are we when we shut hurting people out of the kingdom?

Is being right really more important than being kind? Paul said, "Love is patient; love is kind.… Now faith, hope, and love remain, these three, and the greatest of these is love" (1 Cor 13:4, 13).

Blaming Others

A wise observer said, "Golfers blame their poor performance on sorry golf clubs. Presidents blame bad economic conditions on the previous administration. Workers blame low productivity on the guy in the next department. We almost never say, 'I didn't succeed because I wasn't willing to put forth the effort.'"

Many people claim to be a self-made success, but few say, "I'm a self-made failure." We take credit for our successes and blame others for our failures. Someone said, "Success has a thousand fathers, but failure is an orphan."

When we feel hostility toward someone, it's usually because they remind us of something we hate in ourselves! Attacking others is about as silly as breaking a mirror because you don't like the reflection you see. Notice when the prodigal son got home, he said, "I have sinned! Nobody else is to blame for my predicament but me."

He could have said, "I had an overindulgent father. He had no business giving me all my inheritance. He should have known I would waste it."

He could have said, "You don't know how tough it is to be the baby of the family. My older brother is so jealous. He made life miserable for me."

Instead, he said, "No! It's not my father; it's not my brother; it's not my home situation. I'm to blame. I have sinned!"

Paul says, "Each one of us will be held accountable" (Rom 14:12).

Blessed Are the Peacemakers

Discord and animosity abound today. Even our language reflects that attitude. Politicians and lawyers promise to *fight* for your interests. Religious leaders criticize the *wrong* beliefs of other faiths. Businesses try to *outsell* their competitors. Sports teams stress *crushing* their opponents. Radio talk show hosts and newspaper columnists use sarcasm and ridicule when dealing with those who disagree. Social media is vicious!

Something is drastically wrong. We seem to be adrenaline addicts and conflict junkies. We are attracted to violent events. We watch violent movies, read violent books, and play violent videogames. These practices are dangerous in a world full of weapons.

In a democracy we should be able to express our beliefs and opinions without condemning other people's beliefs and opinions. As responsible citizens and concerned Christians we must not encourage those candidates or leaders who constantly belittle their opponents. In fact, we should never buy objects, attend events, or listen to diatribes that offer more noise than light. To live peacefully in a small world, logical discussions must take precedence over emotional tirades.

The psalmist said, "How very good and pleasant it is when kindred live together in unity!" (Ps 133:1).

Paul said, "If it is possible, so far as it depends on you, live peaceably with all" (Rom 12:18).

Jesus said, "Blessed are the peacemakers, for they will be called children of God" (Matt 5:9).

Building Up or Tearing Down?

It takes years to build a great structure, but it only takes a few minutes to demolish it. The same thing is true of reputations and policies. It's easy to be against something. Fear tactics, criticism, bullying, and threats require no thought or energy. You can arouse a crowd to mob mentality with a few negative labels and emotional insinuations. But you can't build a consensus for progress with these methods.

Creating a productive project is different. That requires solid information, reasonable dialogues, and logical analysis. Unfortunately, these things are not simplistic, catchy, or exciting. Instead, they take time and careful consideration.

That's why many people are taken in by a bumper-sticker mentality, consisting of glib phrases and destructive propaganda. In a democracy it's the "ordinary people" who determine its success or failure. Therefore, ordinary people must disregard emotional hype and become sensible and thoughtful. Anyone can find faults and tear down, but it takes a dedicated, caring person to build up. Paul said, "Encourage one another and build up each other" (1 Thess 5:11).

Never criticize or attack anything unless you are prepared to replace it with something better!

Closing the Gap

In life there is always a gap between what is and what ought to be. There is always a gap between what we have and what we want. There is always a gap between who we are and who we'd like to be. Since gaps cause a state of dissonance and since dissonance causes extreme stress, we are always desperate to close this gap.

There several ways to do this. The first way is to claim there is no gap. We can pretend the two positions are identical: "I wouldn't change a thing"; "This is the best of all possible worlds." Unfortunately, this is usually false. It deludes us, and delusions can't be maintained.

The second way is to pull the ideal level down to the actual level. We can lower our expectations. We can do this by ridiculing intellectuals, condemning our neighbors, and judging our associates. In short, pulling others down to our level is the easy way but not the most productive.

The third way is to raise our actual level to the ideal level. This is the most difficult but also the most productive.

To balance a scale you can either take some weight off the high side or add some weight to the low side. In short, I can lower you or raise me.

Since it's much easier to lower you, insecure people constantly find the flaws and undermine the successes of others. We must realize, however, that these ploys only work temporarily and destructively. The permanent constructive way to close the gap is to raise me by learning, growing, and maturing.

Peter said, "Grow in the grace and knowledge of our Lord and Savior Jesus Christ" (2 Pet 3:18).

Cooperation

An old story illustrates the importance of cooperation:

> A famous Arabian poet was traveling through the desert. The sun became extremely hot, and he was desperate for water. Finally, when he reached an oasis and tried to draw water from the well, he discovered that his rope was not long enough to reach the bottom.
>
> In despair, he was resigned to die when he saw an approaching rider. He wondered if it was a friend or foe. At last, he saw that it was a chieftain of an enemy tribe. Ignoring the dying poet, this man also tried his rope, but it was not long enough to reach the water either.

Now would these enemies choose to cooperate or choose to die? The two were willing to put their hostilities aside and tie their ropes together so both could quench their thirst. Soon, the bucket was brimming with sparkling water.

The lesson is apparent: There is value in cooperation.
Paul says, "Live in harmony with one another" (Rom 15:5).

Cooperation or Confrontation?

As a pluralistic society on a small planet, we all share the same space and use the same resources. We obey universal laws and hold universal values. We pool taxes and enjoy the benefits of public utilities. Therefore, both religious and nonreligious people must find common ground. It's obvious we will have to make compromises. If each group takes an absolute stand on every issue, we're in trouble.

Now, the extremists at each end of the spectrum will probably never be able to meet. But in the interest of peace and progress, most of us realize that a middle position, gained through cooperation, is more productive than confrontation.

So is there anything we can agree on? Since each religion, each culture, and each individual has a different idea of God and a different set of customs and taboos, the situation seems rather hopeless. Fortunately, there are issues of shared agreement. Almost all viable religions and reasonable individuals reverence human life. Almost all cultures in all localities emphasize morals that elevate human welfare. This can give us a basis for productive interaction.

Schools can't teach sectarian doctrines and denominational creeds, but they can teach "love of neighbor." Legislators can't pass laws prohibiting specific "sins," but they can prohibit acts that diminish the quality of human life.

In a democracy, everyone must be given equal opportunity to practice and promote their beliefs. None of us has a right to take unfair advantage of this privilege. Any freedom that I claim for myself must be freely and willingly extended to others. Furthermore, I must do this regardless of how ridiculous or sacrilegious their teachings may seem to me. Jesus said, "Do to others as you would have them do to you" (Matt 7:12).

This broad ideology, based on the ultimate value and dignity of individual human beings, can be the common denominator of a diverse population. It can be accepted by those who espouse any of the world's innumerable religions or even no religion at all.

Cooperation is better than confrontation!

Defensiveness

Some of us have chips on our shoulders that can be knocked off by the slightest breeze. We wouldn't be so touchy if we realized that most of the time, we're not even the target of angry outbursts. We just get caught in the crossfire. Solomon tells us how to handle controversial situations. He said, "A soft answer turns away wrath, but a harsh word stirs up anger" (Prov 15:1).

Every person has his own problems and eccentricities. A cashier told the following story:

> An old man came into the bank, threw down a check, and said, "Cash it!"
>
> I was new, so I said, "I'm sorry, sir, but I'll need some identification."
>
> "Cash it!" the man said a little louder.
>
> The bank's manager hurried to the counter. "This is our college intern," she said, "and he doesn't know our customers yet."
>
> "Just cash the check!" the man snarled.
>
> After that, whenever I saw him come in, I shuddered. My parents told me to be friendly. I tried. "Good morning, Mr. Kempis. How are you today?"
>
> "Fine. Cash the check."
>
> "Great day, Mr. Kempis. Got any plans?"
>
> "Nothing special. Cash the check."
>
> One morning, I was startled to hear, "Good morning!"
>
> It was Mr. Kempis, and he was smiling. I was stunned. Later, I learned his wife had been undergoing cancer treatment. Now she was better, and Mr. Kempis was happy. All that hostility hadn't had one thing to do with me.

We never know what hidden problems and pains are generating hateful words and rude actions from others. Often, it has absolutely nothing to do with us.

Democracy

"Muslims aren't loyal citizens"' "Atheists don't have rights!"; "Those who refuse to salute the flag should be jailed!"; "Down with deviants!"

Such statements are common and even popular among sincere but misguided patriots. Unfortunately, they reveal total ignorance of democracy and all it stands for.

Let's paraphrase Jesus's admonition: "If you love those who love you, what reward do you have? Do not even the tax collectors do the same?" (Matt 5:46).

Likewise, if you only allow freedom of expression for those who agree with you, of what virtue is that? Any dictator or repressive regime does that. The genius and greatness of a democracy is that it allows freedom of expression, even for those who disagree with it!

A great man captured the essence of democracy when he said, "I don't agree with one word you say, but I'll defend to the death your right to say it."

Few of us are that wise and mature, but our future as a nation depends upon it. Unless all of us are free, soon none of us will be free!

Deny, Distort, or Distract

Manipulators are constantly seeking our allegiance and support. They use sneaky, clever methods to influence us. When we point out their illogical beliefs or immoral standards, their first defense is to deny the accusations and declare, "I didn't say that" or "You are mistaken."

If we insist our statement is true and offer proof of their deceit, they quickly move to distortion. They put a spin on the situation by twisting the data, changing word definitions, and claiming it's been taken out of context. This can cause such confusion that it almost makes us doubt our own sanity.

If we hang tough, relying on reason and presenting evidence, they will soon move to distraction by changing the subject entirely. They may do this by creating an emergency or instigating a chaotic incident. In fact, they will point out any shiny object of interest far removed from the matter at hand.

We must not fall for any of these ploys. When we are dealing with people who have ulterior motives—such as opponents who want to win, salesmen who want our money, or politicians who want our votes—we must be vigilant and wise. The scripture never advises Christians to be gullible or naive. Instead, Jesus said, "Be wise as serpents and innocent as doves" (Matt 10:16).

Don't Burn Your Bridges

Don't burn your bridges. Someone else may still need to cross the creek.

When we grow beyond certain beliefs and practices, it becomes tempting to ridicule, repudiate, and attack them. The first-grader despises the preschooler. The teenager despises the elementary student. The rich despise the poor.

Sometimes when we increase in knowledge and understanding, we tend to become arrogant and forget our past.

A boy with a broken leg will eventually be able to lay his crutches aside. Even so, he has no right to destroy them, because other injured people may need them.

Likewise, it's wonderful to become mature enough and healthy enough to lay aside certain immature religious beliefs and customs. The aids and crutches may actually impede our progress at our present level of development, but we must realize other people may still need them.

If you are climbing a tower and reach level two, you may be finished with the ladder below, but don't destroy it. Other folks are still on level one. In fact, some climbers are probably already on level three! They are finished with the ladder below them, but you'd better hope they didn't destroy it, because that's the very ladder you need now!

You see, all things are relative. None of us has already arrived at "truth." Therefore, ridiculing any person's beliefs or practices is more than rude. It's wrong! Just because you have no further need for a thing doesn't give you the right to destroy it!

Paul tells us to "encourage the fainthearted, help the weak, be patient with all of them" (1 Thess 5:14).

Don't Overreact

Many of us overreact to any supposed slights or criticisms. Revenge and retaliation cause more problems than they cure. In fact, fighting evil usually does more harm than good. One lady said, "My neighbor was painting her house one day. I came by and saw big splashes of fresh red paint speckled all over her white garage doors. 'What happened?' I asked. She smiled ruefully. 'Well, I was painting the patio bench when a moth began fluttering around. I swatted at it with my brush—and this is the result. I shouldn't have let a little insect aggravate me like that.'"

Our reactions often make things worse. Many things should just be overlooked and forgotten. Life is too short to make mountains out of molehills. We need to ask, "Will this matter a year from now?" We need to evaluate what an issue is worth in terms of our peace of mind.

Our overreactions often backfire: "Old Mr. Jones had fished the river for years. He always carried his shotgun, along with his fishing rod. One afternoon, he edged his boat under a tangle of brush and was almost asleep when he heard an ominous thud. A water moccasin had dropped off a limb into his boat. In a panic, he snatched up his shotgun and blasted the snake, but he also blew the bottom out of his boat and had to be rescued from the river."

We often do that when we overreact to some incident. We destroy not only the evil that threatens us but much good as well. It's like burning down a house to kill a rat. Paul said, "See that none of you repays evil for evil, but always seek to do good to one another" (1 Thess 5:15).

Egocentricity

Every living organism is somewhat egocentric because selfishness is a survival instinct. To every child, the time is *now*; the place is *here*; the person is *me*!

Being egocentric means *my* sore toe is much more important to me than a famine in Bangladesh or an earthquake in China. This is normal, and it can even be positive in a crisis, but eventually we must grow beyond it.

Many primitive instincts were once necessary for our survival, but as we mature, we must find more humane and productive ways to respond. Paul said, "Do not seek your own advantage but that of the other" (1 Cor 10:24).

Being egocentric causes pain to those around us. Immature couples divorce to find pleasure and do great injury to children and loved ones. Some people drink or do drugs and say, "It's my body and my business." But no man is an island. Everything we do affects our family and friends and community.

Unselfishness is essential for both maturity and sanity. A psychologist said, "The first mark of recovery in a mental patient is when he begins to show concern for other people."

Jesus said, "The Son of Man came not to be served but to serve" (Matt 20:28).

Enabling

Enabling is destructive because it teaches false lessons. It rewards unproductive behavior, and it creates dependency.

When we intervene between actions and their consequences, we are undermining the lessons life is trying to teach. Tough love allows some pain now to avoid worse pain later. When the eagles teach their young to fly, their methods seem cruel. They urge the little ones out of the nest and nudge them off the edge. It's a "fly or die" situation, but none die! This tough love motivates them to do what birds must do naturally. If you take away their necessity for flying, they won't learn, and they'll be crippled for life.

Paul was clear about enabling. He said, "Anyone unwilling to work should not eat" (2 Thess 3:10).

Years ago, cars often had to be pushed before they would start, but that didn't mean people were obligated to push them all the way from California to New York City. The cars were expected to become autonomous after a little help. It's the same with people.

When we reward unproductive behavior, we are setting the stage for disaster. Monterey, California, once had a thriving fishing industry. There was also a huge colony of pelicans nearby. These birds usually feed themselves by swooping low over the water and scooping up fish in their bills. But these pelicans didn't have to do that. They could eat their fill of the fish heads that were being dropped over the sides of the fishing boats. They had it made. Food was provided.

They were all well fed and happy. Then, unexpectedly, the cannery closed, and these pelicans had a problem. By then, a whole generation of birds didn't know how to fish. They hadn't learned because they had been enabled. The birds began to starve. Many died.

Enabling creates indolence, and indolence is deadly. Enabling also hurts the ones who enable. It wastes their resources and eventually causes them to become resentful and bitter.

Enmeshment

In enmeshed families there are no boundaries between what's me and what's not me. We lose touch with our feelings because they have been discounted. When we were children, adults said, "Oh, you don't really hate your aunt!" or "You're not really afraid of that little spider!" We're told we shouldn't be happy if our sister is sad. We're made to feel ashamed for something an uncle did. After years of this, we become so entwined with our families and associates that we don't know where we end and they begin. We don't even know what desires and interests and responsibilities are our own.

The lives in enmeshed families are like a tangled mass of electrical cords. Each person gives up his uniqueness and plays his rigid role to be loyal to the system. Any attempt to be different is met with anger and rejection. A member of a dysfunctional family who has different interests and beliefs is often made to feel a neurotic sense of guilt. In fact, the individuals in a dysfunctional family exist only for the family.

Jesus exerted his individuality, even at the age of twelve. When his mother rebuked him for staying in the temple, he answered quite sharply for a child of that time: "His mother said to him, 'Child, why have you treated us like this? Your father and I have been anxiously looking for you.' He said to them, 'Why were you searching for me? Did you not know that I must be in my Father's house?'" (Luke 2:48–49).

Also, he was abrupt and adamant when his family interrupted his ministry. The scriptures say, "While he was still speaking to the crowds, his mother and his brothers were standing outside, wanting to speak to him. Someone told him, 'Look, your mother and your brothers are standing outside, wanting to speak to you.' But to the one who had told him this, Jesus replied, 'Who is my mother, and who are my brothers?' And pointing to his disciples, he said, 'Here are my mother and my brothers!'" (Matt 12:46–49).

Jesus wasn't enmeshed: "My mother and my brothers are those who hear the word of God and do it" (Luke 8:21).

Forgiving Ourselves and Others

Have you ever had a bad experience? Have you ever been cheated? Have you ever been treated unfairly?

Of course you have! Everyone has. But are any of these bad experiences still affecting your life? Are they still limiting your productivity? Are they still stifling your growth?

Isn't it time to let them go? Haven't you hurt enough? It's true that Jesus said to "forgive seventy-seven times," but he also commanded us to let go: "If anyone will not welcome you or listen to your words, shake off the dust from your feet as you leave that house or town" (Matt 10:14).

When we've made a mistake and apologized, that's all we can do. If the person refuses to reconcile, then there comes a time when we need to say, "Well, that's that. I've grieved long enough. I've cried and lost sleep long enough. I've been depressed and guilty long enough. It's time to put this matter away and begin living again." That's what shaking the dust off your feet is all about.

This may sound insensitive, but it's not! We can't allow ourselves to be held hostage to remorse forever. At some point we have to say, "It's time to go on."

And what about a person who has hurt you? You have to let that go too. Striking back won't help. Hanging around to be a convenient target for continued rejection and abuse won't help either. There comes a time to "shake the dust from your feet" and move on.

We need to forgive others so we can live without debilitating bitterness, and we need to forgive ourselves and "shake the dust off our feet" when others refuse to forgive us.

The Hero Syndrome

Everyone admires a hero. Firemen, policeman, soldiers, and even ordinary citizens are honored for saving lives. It's normal and positive to enjoy helping people, but it can get out of control. If individuals become addicted to the "rescue role," a dangerous obsession can develop. Then, if not enough natural events provide opportunities for them to "play the hero," they may create their own opportunities.

There is a mental illness called Munchausen's Syndrome in which parents injure their children and then rush them to the emergency room for treatment. These sick people receive a double payoff. They act out their latent hostilities by inflicting pain, and then they are praised for their care and concern.

This also plays itself out in psychological areas. Those who have a strong need to be a hero may abuse their spouse and then comfort them. They may set up their partners to fail and then rush in and help them succeed. They may even encourage infidelity and then become the "saintly forgiver."

This is a complex and perverted pattern that's difficult to detect. It's terribly destructive to victims because they do not suspect what's happening.

So be a hero and enjoy helping, but realize there are plenty of hurting people. You don't need to create them. Paul said, "Do not use your freedom as an opportunity for self-indulgence" (Gal 5:13).

Honest Speech

To communicate, we must be honest, clear, and personal. We must use "I" language to describe how we really feel and explain what we really want. Leveling is saying things like, "I really care about you" or "I feel hurt when you tease me" or "I'm afraid you won't love me if I reveal my thoughts."

The Bible is critical of deceitful speech. The psalmist said evil people will deceive us with "speech smoother than butter but with a heart set on war" (Ps 55:21).

Honest speech means being sincere and open. People who deceive and lie and fail to admit their true motives will never be trusted, and they will never be able to develop intimate relationships. Many people are reluctant to level with others because they are afraid to face the truth about themselves. Sometimes we've pretended and postured and played the hypocrite so long that we don't really know our own deep desires and values. Communication is ten percent about facts and ninety percent about feelings. We must relate heart to heart as well as head to head.

Secrets are deadly. It's almost always better to express things than to deny or suppress them.

How to Win

Suppose a "know-it-all" walks up to you and says, "I hear you're a teacher. Well, all teachers are lazy slobs."

Now, you have several options: You can hit him. You can walk away. You can say, "You're crazy," and start an argument. Or you can stand firm, look calm, and say absolutely nothing.

He will be surprised, but he'll probably continue: "That fellow was right when he said, 'They've just got book learnin' and no common sense.'"

Refuse to refute. Instead, calmly say, "Well, that's one point of view."

Your adversary will blink and clear his throat. He's becoming confused. "Well, the critics ought to know, oughten they?"

Now he's moving from offensive to defensive. Don't bite. Just say, "Go ahead. I'm listening"—and you are listening to find out why he has this attitude. Did some teacher embarrass him? Is he envious of his educated associates? Does he feel guilty because he dropped out of school?

At this point he may shift into neutral and say, "Well, anyhow, some folks think they're overpaid. What do you think?"

That's the signal that you're winning. The attack has fizzled. The guy who wanted to corner you is now asking your opinion. You can leave him disarmed, or you can continue the experiment. Tell him about a teacher who was a misfit and a failure. Admit there are some such cases. This lets him save face. Then say, "But there's another teacher who has helped hundreds of children and even tutors them free of charge. You can hardly say she's a lazy slob."

Since you listened to him, he's now listening to you and agrees she may be a good teacher. He may even conclude he is a little bit prejudiced.

The steps to this astonishing method of avoiding conflict are these: Don't react. Don't contradict. Don't cave in. Maintain "computer mode" attitude. Say, "Tell me more." Most attackers will run out of steam in two or three minutes, and you win!

Remember, Solomon said, "A soft answer turns away wrath, but a harsh word stirs up anger" (Prov 15:1).

Kissing Frogs

There's an old story about a handsome prince who falls under a wicked spell. The prince takes on the form of a frog and is told the only way he can regain his royal potential is to be kissed by a princess.

This isn't just a fairytale. It's an allegory. The world is full of people under a "frog spell." These croaking, nonproductive creatures can be transformed into persons. They can get transformed by a kiss, by a touch, or by a word of acceptance and appreciation.

Jesus never looked at what a person had been but always at what the person could be! He walked the earth as a servant. He washed feet, touched lepers, and paid the ultimate price in death. Then he left his spirit with us so the business of "frog kissing" could continue.

He told us to "go out into the roads and lanes, and compel people to come in" (Luke 14:23).

Labels Are Dangerous

He's a liberal! She's a conservative! These are left wing! Those are right wing! Fundamentalists! Traditionalists! Progressives! Radicals!

It seems everybody is being labeled these days. We toss the terms around so glibly and so absolutely, but such labels are misleading. Perhaps we're we so prone to label those around us because if we can give individuals a neat label, then we can dismiss them. If they are labeled, then all our thinking is done for us. We can agree or disagree with them on the basis of a preconceived prejudice rather than on the basis of reason. We can love them or hate them on the basis of prescribed rules rather than on personal merit.

The only problem with this prevalent practice is that most labels are totally false! In fact, everyone is liberal on some things and conservative on other things. Everyone is a "fundamentalist" if you will let them define the fundamentals! We may be ultratraditional when it comes to marriage customs but ultramodern when it comes to buying a computer or an appliance.

Also, it's ironic that the people who lambast "compromises" in theological areas may be the very ones who practice the epitome of compromise in business areas. For instance, groups who attack their own members for slightly diverse views may champion their former enemies in political battles.

It seems that the ends justify the means if I need to use them. It seems compromise is fine if I do it but sinful if you do it. It seems personal opinions are convictions if I believe them but heresy if you believe them!

Carelessly applying derogatory labels amounts to name-calling. This is unacceptable in a democratic society. These cheap prejudicial labels do nothing to clarify complex issues. Calling anyone who disagrees with me an unpatriotic, antifamily atheist is unfair and destructive.

In short, we must not use labels that foster ignorance and animosity. Instead, we must be a reasonable voice amid the irrational clamor.

Paul said, "Let no evil talk come out your mouths but only what is good for building up" (Eph 4:29).

Last Things

We quote famous last words. We hear of last rites. We read last wills and testaments. There's always a last time for everything; unfortunately, we're usually unaware of it.

For instance, there will be a last time to see that friend, a last phone call from your dad, a last family reunion, a last Christmas together, or a last worship service. At some point we'll plant our last garden, buy our last pair of shoes, go to our last movie, and eat our last hamburger. We take all these things for granted because we do them every day. We feel the future is endless and the opportunities are limitless.

How different we might act if we could know when some ordinary event is occurring for the last time. We'd record the words and photograph the people. We'd pay more attention to the details and plan to cherish the memory forever. Instead, when we suddenly realize we'll never again get to experience a certain incident or be with a certain person, we look back in regret. We say, "Oh, if I'd only known!"; "Why didn't I listen more carefully?"; "Why didn't I look more closely?"; "Why didn't I appreciate more deeply?"

Yes, there's a last time for everything. So let's have every conversation as if it were the last. Let's enjoy every visit as if it were the last. Let's live each moment as if it were the last, because someday it will be!

David knew this when he said, "There is but a step between me and death" (1 Sam 20:3).

The Law of Balance

Nature avoids extremes. For instance, tall men and women don't usually produce taller children, and short men and women don't usually produce shorter children. Instead, the genetic lineage tends to move toward the middle. Balance is the key!

Also, controllers rarely seek out and marry other controllers. Instead, people seem to be innately attracted to mates that have opposite or complementary traits. Thus, their offspring tend to move toward the middle. You see, if we as a species kept getting taller and taller, or shorter and shorter, or more and more dominating, we would soon be so aberrant that we wouldn't survive.

The same principle works in social situations. Relationships are like seesaws. The farther one partner moves toward his end of the board, the farther the other partner must move toward the other end of the board to maintain balance. If the wife is a spendthrift, the husband feels compelled to be a miser. The more she spends, the more he saves. If the husband is daring, the wife feels compelled to be cautious. The more he risks, the more timid she becomes. If a mother is permissive, the father feels compelled to be strict. If a father is combative, the mother feels compelled to be conciliatory. If one is a workaholic, the other feels compelled to emphasize recreation. What one condemns, the other feels the need to defend.

All of these are simply attempts to maintain balance in the relationship. Unfortunately, since neither partner is aware of nature's inexorable law of balance, this behavior causes conflict. Each seems to be deliberately contradicting and frustrating the other. But if both realize what's happening, the problem can be solved. Rather than moving toward the extremes to maintain balance, they can each move toward the middle. This will also maintain balance, and it's called compromise and cooperation.

The psalmist explains it this way, saying, "How very good and pleasant it is when kindred live together in unity!" (Ps 133:1).

Listening

Real communication requires information to be both sent and received.

We think we know what others are saying. Too often, however, we don't. Instead of listening, many of us try to read minds or plan our response. A business magazine tells how a dispatcher made a million-dollar error by not listening. He was instructed to route a delivery of building material to Portland. At that point he stopped listening and sent eight truckloads of lumber to Portland, Oregon. It was supposed to go to Portland, Maine.

To be good listeners, we must hear everything people say, and we must not hear anything people don't say. We also need to paraphrase back what we've heard to check whether that's exactly what they meant. Solomon said, "Let the wise, too, hear and gain in learning" (Prov 1:5).

We must hear between the lines. How a person says something can be just as important as what he says. Furthermore, we must note what is not said as well as what is said.

Do we hear the insecurity behind the boasting? Do we hear the hurt behind the angry outburst? Do we hear the deep sadness behind the glib jokes? If not, we have poor listening skills.

Really hearing what others say and having empathy is what one writer calls "holy listening." More than anything else, people want to be heard.

Jesus said, "Listen and understand" (Matt 15:10).

Peaceful Christians

An old hunter said, "One lesson I learned from my dog was that he could kill a skunk, but it wasn't worth the trouble." It's the same with us. In marriage or business dealings or church decisions, fighting over trivial issues and obscure doctrines is like killing a skunk: It's not worth the price you pay.

Today we have spouse abuse, road rage, and gang violence. Such unresolved anger is even causing denominational disputes and church splits. Jesus said, "Be at peace with one another" (Mark 9:50).

An elderly woman said, "When you get old and look back, you realize how much time you wasted being concerned over things that really didn't matter at all. What if my son left the bathroom light on or someone spilled apple juice on the carpet? I remember getting extremely upset over incidents that were so inconsequential."

A talk show host said, "Sometimes when I get bitter letters attacking something I've said, I know that this bitterness is not really directed at me but rather at people who have deeply hurt the writers. When I respond, I tell them I wish I knew what had happened in their past because I'd like to help them. They often answer by saying, "You're right. I had a bitter experience with my parent or a friend, and it has stayed with me all this time."

When people attack you, analyze the situation. See if they are reacting to an old injury, and treat them with understanding.

We're never required to be doormats, but being overly defensive and touchy is unproductive.

We should ignore many trivial aggravations and refuse to take every slight personally. Often, we're just caught in the middle of someone's misplaced anger.

Legend says that once upon a time the hands, the feet, and the mouth said to each other, "We do all the work gathering and chewing food, but that lazy fellow, the stomach, does nothing. It's high time he did some work too, so let's go on strike!" They quit working. They soon began to feel weaker and weaker until at last they realized that the stomach was actually their stomach, and they would have to feed it in order to remain alive.

It's the same with us. As Christians, and even as human beings, we're all in this life together. We must not fight among ourselves. That's deadly! Jesus said, "No city or house divided against itself will stand" (Matt 12:25).

Peace or Conflict?

The Bible begins with Cain killing his brother Abel and ends with a horrifying apocalyptic war with two cultures annihilating each other. Confrontations, conflicts, and disagreements are universal and constant.

The scriptures are filled with examples of relationship problems, such as Jacob and Esau, Joseph and his brothers, David and Saul, Paul and Barnabas. Thousands of biblical verses advocate peace and condemn discord. Jesus told us to love our enemies and offer forgiveness seventy-seven times if necessary. In fact, there are many more passages about these social issues than there are about being born again.

We live in a violent world. News sources inform us of unspeakable horrors every day. After realizing both the emphasis of the gospel and the great needs of humanity, it's unbelievable that churches present so few studies and sermons on how to solve disputes and achieve harmony. Paul said, "God is a God not of disorder but of peace" (1 Cor 14:33).

He also commanded us to "be at peace among yourselves" (1 Thess 5:13).

Both Jesus and the Bible stress love and forgiveness so much because Christians are uniquely qualified to be peacemakers. Since we've been forgiven, we can offer forgiveness. Since we've experienced God's grace, we can extend that grace to others. It's an absolute tragedy when we see hatred and dissension within churches and congregations.

Remember, Jesus was introduced to this world with a message of peace. The angels sang, "Glory to God in the highest heaven, and on earth peace among those whom he favors!" (Luke 2:14).

Jesus also said, "Blessed are the peacemakers, for they will be called children of God" (Matt 5:9).

People Skills

Ninety percent of people who lose their jobs are fired because they have poor people skills. Most of us are so egocentric and insecure that we point fingers to avoid blame. We put others down to make ourselves look better. Jesus said, "Love your enemies…that you may be children of your Father in heaven, for he makes his sun rise on the evil and on the good and sends rain on the righteous and on the unrighteous" (Matt 5:44–45).

God offers his love and support to all people, and so should we. That doesn't mean we must agree with everyone or condone their actions or even have affection for them. That's neither productive nor possible. But we're to have agape love, which means concern for their well-being. This kind of love includes respect, justice, and compassion.

We're all different, and that's okay!

A group of art students were sketching a river scene. The students were spread out along the bank, so each one was viewing from a slightly different perspective. The scene itself was the same, but the perceptions and interpretations were different. No critic could say that one sketch was right and the others were wrong. They were just different!

It's the same with people. Each of us views life from a different perspective; therefore, our opinions and descriptions are not alike. That doesn't mean they are wrong. It just means they are different.

Please Don't Agree or Disagree

When we hear a person give an opinion, share an idea, or state a belief, why do most of us feel obligated to either agree or disagree? Wouldn't it be wonderful if we could realize these are not the only two possible reactions? In fact, these are often inappropriate and nonproductive reactions.

Suppose a group is standing around watching Old Faithful erupt. One person says, "Oh, the sun's reflection on the water makes a beautiful red and blue rainbow." Would a person over on the other side immediately reply, "That's not true!" or "That's wrong!"? Of course not!

Instead, the person might say, "How interesting. From here it looks yellow and green!" or "You know, from this angle it's almost a silhouette!" or "I see an entirely different reflection."

In short, the listeners in this case would feel no urge to either verify or repudiate the speaker's comment. They would realize views from different angles do look different. They would realize they can't see the whole thing from their particular position. So they would simply hear it and add their own insights.

Why can't we be that sensible in other areas of discussion instead of feeling threatened and becoming defensive?

If a person gives an opinion, shares an idea, or states a belief, we don't have to agree or disagree. We don't have to verify it or repudiate it. Indeed, we really can't verify it or repudiate it! We can't "see it" for him. Instead, we can simply hear and add our own insights. If we do that, then both of us will know more about the subject. He'll know how it looks to us, and we'll know how it looks to him.

Most issues have so many aspects that none of us can see them all. When people look at things from different perspectives, it's natural for them to give different descriptions. We must realize that two different views are not necessarily mutually exclusive! They may both be valid! Life and truth are not contests based on the principle that if you win, I lose; or if you're right, I'm wrong! On the contrary, the more we can learn about the "other sides" of life that are hidden from us or out of our line of sight, the more accurate our perception will be.

The only way we can ever fully understand anything is to perceive it from every possible viewpoint. Therefore, the next time you hear a person give an opinion, share an idea, or state a belief, don't agree or disagree! Just hear it, evaluate it, keep any useful information, and let the rest go!

Solomon gives us advice: "Listen to advice and accept instruction, that you may gain wisdom for the future" (Prov 19:20).

Projection

Jesus understood the principle of projection. The flaws and weaknesses that ignorant and insecure individuals are constantly pointing out in others are really the flaws and weaknesses they have deep within their own makeup.

Paul clearly warned us about projecting, saying, "When you judge others… you condemn yourself, because you, the judge, are doing the very same things" (Rom 2:1).

In other words, the problems you see in others are inevitably the problems you have in your own life.

Unfortunately, the individuals who do this don't usually realize what they are doing. Knowledgeable people, however, are immediately aware that these negative and miserable people are revealing much more about themselves than they are about those they are attacking.

For instance, if a critic says, "You are a liar," he's really saying, "I know I would be lying in this situation."

If he says, "You are as dumb as a doorknob," he's really saying, "I have serious doubts about my own intelligence."

If he says, "You are crooked and deceitful," he's really saying, "I know I would be willing to twist the truth, if necessary, to accomplish my goals."

So, you see, projection is a dangerous practice. In fact, it's self-defeating. Instead of diminishing others, the person is actually disclosing hidden flaws and weaknesses about himself!

Propaganda

Propaganda is a way to brainwash large groups of people in short periods of time. Propaganda tells individuals *what* to think instead of teaching them *how* to think. Successful propaganda has four characteristics:

- It is simplistic. It must be popular, and it must be aimed at the lowest and most limited intellectual level.
- It is repetitious. Anything said often enough will be believed. It must have few points, and they must be repeated.
- It is emotional. It must tell people what they want to hear, and it must appeal to their feelings rather than their reason.
- It is one-sided. Everything is absolutely right or wrong. There are no gray areas, and that leaves no room for discussion or dissent.

It's the purpose of propagandists to influence the masses to agree with their position. It is not the purpose of propagandists to discover or propagate truth. Therefore, when you hear politicians or religious leaders give simplistic answers, repeat catchy slogans, ridicule other viewpoints, or tap into your guilts and prejudices, be suspicious. Avoid such situations, or develop resistance to their pressure.

Jesus warned against propaganda. He said, "Beware of false prophets, who come to you in sheep's clothing but inwardly are ravenous wolves" (Matt 7:15).

Recognition and Appreciation

When a TV station cancelled a certain program, they began receiving angry letters. One fan demanded, "Why did you cancel that show? It was the best one you had!"

The manager of the station asked, "Did you ever tell us that?"

"No," he acknowledged, "but I guess I should have."

There's a lesson here: We should never wait until it's too late to show our appreciation. If we're grateful to the man who faithfully sets up the folding chairs, adjusts the thermostat, and locks the doors of our church every week, we should say so.

Each of us begins life with a tremendous need for approval, and we never outgrow this need. Children try to get the attention of an adult by shouting, "Watch me! Watch me!" Throughout our lives, we all continue to say this, but not out loud. Imagine an invisible sign on everyone's chest that reads, "Please notice me! Make me feel important!" We should develop the habit of expressing appreciation. We'll never know the difference that could make in someone's life.

What a loss to think a compliment and not express it. It's a simple yet significant thing to praise a neighbor's garden, a mechanic's skills, a postman's dependability or a child's accomplishments. Unfortunately, the average person utters four times as many criticisms as compliments. It's natural to see flaws and faults and imperfections, but as Christians we can train ourselves to notice every positive thing that happens around us. Showing appreciation and giving sincere compliments can make a real difference in the atmosphere at home, at work, and at church.

Paul advises us to be grateful and appreciative. He said, "Give thanks in all circumstances, for this is the will of God" (1 Thess 5:18).

Righteous Indignation

The psalmist says, "Refrain from anger and forsake wrath…. It leads only to evil" (Ps 37:8).

Yet the scriptures also say of Jesus that "he looked around at them with anger" (Mark 3:5).

Anger is neither good nor bad. It is neither right nor wrong. It can be useful or harmful. It can be constructive or destructive.

We all get angry at times. But if our anger happens too often, is too intense, or lasts too long, it's wrong. Some things aren't worth fighting over, and we have to learn to conserve our strength for the important issues.

There is a rare and unselfish anger known as "righteous indignation." This isn't caused by personal hurts, embarrassments, or fears. It's caused by concern for others! Social injustice, human suffering, and willful ignorance can provoke anger in sensitive and caring individuals.

Jesus was angry for those who couldn't be angry for themselves. He was angry for the oppressed, the helpless, the children, the prisoners, and the slaves of this world.

The Bible calls this kind of anger "God's wrath." Unfortunately, our own anger is much more likely to be over petty personal affronts. As Christians we must not treat minor annoyances as significant issues! Anger is too often self-destructive.

A thirsty lion and a thirsty water buffalo arrived at an oasis. They argued about who would drink first. Soon, they became so enraged that they were determined to fight to the death. Then they looked up and saw a flock of vultures hovering overhead, waiting for the loser to fall. Their quarrel was quickly resolved when they realized that a little cooperation was better than the alternative.

Scams and Victims

Cons and scams, like almost everything else, require "two to tango." There must be a "predator" and a "prey."

The predators, with manipulative tendencies, have certain characteristics that can be detected: They are self-centered and lack empathy; they're inconsistent, saying one thing and doing another; they are long on talk and short on accomplishment; they start many projects and finish nothing; they are grandiose instead of realistic.

Unfortunately, the prey, with a victim mentality, are at risk. They also have certain characteristics that make them vulnerable: They want something for nothing; they need approval and can't say, "No!" they fear confrontation; they may be overly submissive; they have low self-esteem and are susceptible to guilt.

Predators can sense those with a victim mentality, and they gather like vultures around a weak animal. Jesus knew this when he said, "Do not give what is holy to dogs, and do not throw your pearls before swine, or they will trample them under foot and then turn and maul you" (Matt 7:6).

Remember if something sounds too good to be true, it probably is! Don't be gullible. Jesus said, "I am sending you out like sheep into the midst of wolves, so be wise as serpents and innocent as doves" (Matt 10:16).

Seesaws or Elevators?

For me to go up, you must go down! This is known as the seesaw theory of social relationships. It's a popular, logical-sounding theory; unfortunately, it's totally false and destructive.

This philosophy causes me to criticize you. It turns me into a self-righteous hypocrite. It makes me hide my faults and magnify yours. If I can only go up when you go down and you can only go up if I go down, then putting each other down becomes an obsession. This creates a hostile and nonproductive atmosphere.

Now, seesaws do operate like that, but relationships don't. Instead, social relationships operate on the elevator theory. If you go down, then I go down with you. For me to go up, I must let you go up with me. This philosophy encourages tolerance, cooperation, and goodwill. If we're going up or down together, then putting each other up will become mutually rewarding. This creates a loving and productive atmosphere. That's why it's important to remember that when it comes to relationships, we're on an elevator, not a seesaw!

Paul says, "Love one another with mutual affection; outdo one another in showing honor" (Rom 12:10).

Spare the Rod and Spoil the Child

Over the years we've heard strict authoritarians say, "Spare the rod and spoil the child" (see Prov 13:24), which, by the way, is a misquotation. Why do we hear this so often when there are many other Old Testament admonitions concerning discipline that aren't quoted? Consider this example: "If someone has a stubborn and rebellious son who will not obey his father and mother…then his father and his mother shall take hold of him and bring him out to the elders of his town at the gate of that place…. Then all the men of the town shall stone him to death" (Deut 21:18–19, 21).

Did you know that was in the Bible? Probably not, because it's so outrageous that we ignore it. Why, then, do we keep (mis)quoting, "Spare the rod and spoil the child"?

We do this to justify our own less-than-desirable motives and behavior. You see, we are human beings, and kids can be aggravating. Since we are bigger than they are, we can hit them and relieve our anger. Soon, however, we begin to feel guilty. We know at a deeper level that the punishment was more for us than for them. Therefore, we misquote a scripture to justify our abuse.

It's unfortunate that we hear "spare the rod and spoil the child" much more frequently than we hear Paul's advice: "Fathers, do not provoke your children to anger, but bring them up in the discipline and instruction of the Lord" (Eph 6:4).

He also says, "Fathers, do not provoke your children, or they may lose heart" (Col 3:21).

Furthermore, we don't often hear how Jesus feels about child abuse. But he said, "If any of you cause one of these little ones who believe in me to sin, it would be better for you if a great millstone were hung around your neck and you were thrown into the sea" (Mark 9:42).

He also said, "Unless you change and become like children, you will never enter the kingdom of heaven" (Matt 18:3). Jesus thought we should be trying to become more like little children, who are free of hatred and greed, instead of trying to force little children to become like us!

Now, if parents were perfect, they might be able to administer just and productive corporal punishment, but they aren't perfect! It's impossible for men and women to react without letting their own perversions and hang-ups influence their reaction. After all, *discipline* means "teaching," not "hitting." Besides, the rod mentioned was the shepherd's rod, and no shepherd ever used his rod to beat his sheep. Instead, he used his rod to guide and protect them.

One day, hitting children will be viewed with as much dismay as the once-accepted practice of stoning young people to death is today.

Steps in the Right Direction

When should we affirm and reward people? Should we wait until they have done everything we want them to do? Should we wait until they completely measure up to our standards? Should we wait until they reach absolute perfection?

Many people feel this way. Parents are afraid they'll be settling for mediocrity if they compliment a child for making a B. Coaches are afraid they'll be encouraging laxity if they compliment their players for slight improvements. Nations are afraid they'll be condoning a repressive regime if they compliment a leader for a slight move toward democratization.

This is unrealistic. If you wait for perfection, you'll never affirm anyone. Furthermore, affirmation motivates progress. It's the single best way to move a person toward a goal.

We must realize that those individuals or groups we are trying to change have their own personal and social limitations. Sometimes, slow and steady wins the race. The person or nation may not be all we wish them to be, but if they're better than they were before, then our best response is to give them some encouragement, approval, and time.

So when should we affirm and reward people? We should do it when they take the first step in the right direction! This will strengthen them to take the next step. Half a loaf is better than none, and whole loaves are hard to come by.

The writer of Hebrews says, "Exhort one another every day…so that none of you may be hardened by the deceitfulness of sin" (Heb 3:13).

Tennis or Golf?

Tennis players spend all their time and energy knocking balls back and forth over a net. Their objective is not to get anywhere. Rather, their objective is to react to their opponent.

Golfers, on the other hand, play for themselves. They set their goals and are free to reach them as quickly as possible. Their actions are not determined or affected by their opponents' actions.

Likewise, in life many people spend all their time and energy knocking issues back and forth over a net. Their objective in these nonproductive conflicts is not to get anywhere. Players in these social and religious tennis games have no agendas of their own. Instead, they simply react to others. The rules of their game require them to be against whatever their antagonists are for and for whatever their antagonists are against. Since neither side has positive plans or purposes, they accomplish absolutely nothing. Each merely cancels the other out!

Achievers, on the other hand, are different. They play for themselves. They set their own goals and are free to reach them as quickly as possible. Their actions are not affected by their opponents' actions. In our personal golf game we may hit a hole-in-one, or we may land in the rough. In either case the results are up to us. We're autonomous and self-directing.

As long as we continue to let our opponents call the shots and set our agendas, we'll continue to cancel each other out! We'll continue to expend our time and energy in futile tennis games. Instead, let's play for ourselves. Let's set our own goals and determine to reach them as quickly as possible.

Paul said, "I press on toward the goal" (Phil 3:14).

This Is How It Looks to Me

Every time I read a magazine article or a letter to the editor that's hard-hitting, thought-provoking, or written from an unusual angle, I almost cringe because I know the next issue of that magazine or newspaper will be filled with irate letters of refutation.

Why do people feel so compelled to argue? None of us knows exactly how things are! None of us has examined every aspect of life. So why are we threatened when another person sees or emphasizes something different?

Each individual has a right and indeed an obligation to say, "This is how it looks to me!" Then other people have a right to respond with, "I've also seen and experienced that!" or "I have never seen or experienced that!" or "I'm not sure whether I've seen or experienced that!" What nobody has a right to say is, "You don't see or experience that!" or "You don't have a right to express the things you've seen or experienced."

Why can't we just hear or read and learn? Why can't we realize we don't have to believe or accept every concept that's presented? Expressions of opinions don't change truth! Descriptions of viewpoints don't affect reality! Off base or inadequate concepts won't contaminate us! Spoken or written expressions simply represent one speaker's or writer's personal thoughts and outlooks at the moment. Listeners and readers can either profit from them or dismiss them as irrelevant.

Instead, there's a constant barrage of attacks and counterattacks. It's obvious that we can't make progress if we're constantly reacting! If I'm busy trying to prove that the way it looks to you is wrong, then I don't have the time or energy to discover or relate that this is how it looks to me! Jesus said, "Take the log out of your own eye, and then you will see clearly to take the speck out of your neighbor's eye" (Matt 7:5).

Furthermore, such a confrontational atmosphere stifles growth. Sensitive people are often reluctant to share their perspective because they know they'll be subjected to a vicious onslaught of criticism. Thus, many valid insights are being lost.

Two Plus Two Isn't Four!

A first-grader said, "Today, my teacher told us that 'two plus two is four.'"

"Well, then, she's wrong," his friend replied, "because my teacher said, 'Three plus one is four!'"

A fight ensued as each claimed supremacy for his favorite instructor.

Now, let's analyze this situation. Rules were broken, time was wasted, hurts were inflicted, and friendships were lost all because of ignorance! These children assumed that if two statements are different, then one of them has to be wrong! Let's not judge these children too harshly, however, because everyone, young and old alike, falls prey to this illogical assumption.

This either/or dichotomy is deadly! The idea that things are always absolutely right or wrong is a fallacious assumption. In fact, there are many right ways of viewing truth. There are many right ways of expressing truth. In this case two plus two is four, but three plus one is also four. Furthermore, four plus zero is four, and seven minus three is four, and five minus one is four.

Of course, both teachers were right, even though their statements were entirely different. The equations they gave, plus many others, are perfectly acceptable and correct ways of presenting this particular truth.

When will we ever learn? Relationships are shattered, marriages destroyed, denominations split, and nations torn by war all because of one fallacious assumption! The assumption is this: If you and I are different, then one of us has to be wrong! That's not true!

The next time you hear an opinion or an explanation or a belief that's new or different, don't be defensive! Remember these silly kids fighting over two plus two and three plus one!

Be mature! Be logical! Be wise!

Solomon said, "[Make] your ear attentive to wisdom and [incline] your heart to understanding" (Prov 2:2).

This is the way to gain insight.

The Whole Story

In almost every marriage or relationship problem, one person is labeled as the "controller." These controllers are criticized as the "tyrant." To outside observers they appear as egotists and dictators. Their partners, on the other hand, are usually nice, easygoing individuals who enjoy a lot of sympathy. Everybody likes them. They seem to be getting a raw deal from their cruel partners.

That's how it looks! But that may not be the whole story. Remember, "It takes two to tango," and for every controller there is a controlee. Besides, there's always a reason for relationship patterns. So before we judge, let's analyze the situation.

First, the controller role is not a bed of roses. It's tough! Controllers usually make the plans, correct the mistakes, and work twice as hard as anyone else. They live under constant tension and never relax. They take total responsibility and therefore get most of the blame for failure. Nobody would choose this lifestyle because it's easy or pleasant. Instead, controllers do it because they feel it's necessary.

Second, the controlee role is not all bad. They don't have to plan because the good old controller does it for them. They don't have to exercise caution because the good old controller does it for them. They don't have to take responsibility because the good old controller does it for them. They can relax, take time off, and coast along comfortably.

As a result, they are socially acceptable and popular. Furthermore, they are not really out of control. These types are often "passive-aggressive controllers." That means they do get their way through a roundabout process. When confronted, they smile and agree. When decisions are to be made, they remain quiet. When agendas are discussed, they seem to acquiesce. But when it comes to actual compliance, they evade, procrastinate, dig in their heels, and gradually shape things to suit themselves.

Also, they can punish the controller very effectively. They know all his frustration buttons and push them regularly. For instance, they "lose" the checkbook and therefore come up overdrawn. They "forget" to service the car and therefore can't run an errand. They "spill their coke" at the last minute and have to change clothes—thereby making the controller late for an appointment. Now, of course, these constant "accidents" are always perfectly legitimate, so you can't really blame them.

Finally, there is no way to accurately evaluate the controller and the controlee because you can't know for sure how that marriage or that business or that project would have turned out if the controller had not been in charge. Would there have been financial disaster, social problems, or even criminal consequences? Since we don't know, we must admit, as in most things, there is no absolute villain and no absolute victim. Both play a role, and both get something from the role they play. They enable each other. In fact, the whole controller concept is a myth. There are really two controllers in every situation—one that's obvious and one that's not.

Peter gave couples good advice: "Have unity of spirit, sympathy, love for one another, a tender heart, and a humble mind" (1 Pet 3:8).

Wolves Need Sheep

Every phenomenon has a cause! Criminals must have victims. Predators must have prey. Hawks need chickens. Foxes need rabbits. Cats need mice.

If you have a vacuum in your life, some manipulator will rush in to fill it at your expense. If you are vulnerable, someone will take advantage of that fact. If there were no gullible believers, there would be no perpetrators of nonsense. If there were no lackadaisical dupes, there would be no autocratic dictators. If there were no irresponsible followers, there would be no unscrupulous leaders. In short, if you won't think for yourself, there are plenty of shysters out there quite willing to do it for you—for a price!

Weak, sick, or uncertain animals invite a hostile takeover. They send a clear, unmistakable signal to would-be predators. The message says, "We're vulnerable—a prize for the taking." Likewise, ignorant, lazy, or insecure people send clear, unmistakable signals to would be predators. Furthermore, a large, easily available food source ensures the multiplication of these predators.

If this is true, then fortifying the prey will eventually eradicate the predators. Without a vulnerable food source, predators cannot exist. So how can we fortify the prey and abolish the "food source"? How can we educate people, strengthen people, and make people less susceptible to "wolves" in deceitful clothing?

We could become less susceptible to religious charlatans, political demagogues, and other scam artists if we followed these guidelines:

• Be aware of people who use ignorance, fear, and hatred as hallmarks of their propaganda.

• Don't succumb to threats. Realize "wolves" can use normal human concerns and anxieties as weapons against us.

• Reject emotional sensationalism. This is always used when logical arguments are weak.

• Bolster your self-esteem.

• Trust your instincts. Use your senses. Think for yourself.

• Be assertive. Ask questions and demand proof.

• Don't be naive and submissive. Become an independent, rational person!

Remember this: If the sheep became strong and smart, the wolves would disappear. Jesus said, "I am sending you out like sheep into the midst of wolves, so be wise as serpents and innocent as doves" (Matt 10:16).

Words

Never have we been so overwhelmed with words. In addition to ordinary conversations, various notions, opinions, and accusations come at us from television, radio, internet, social media, blogs, text messages, and billboards. Furthermore, with free speech there are few constraints. Almost anything can be said! These rumors and innuendos are usually more false than true, more negative than positive, and more harmful than helpful. Too many words come from foolish people.

Furthermore, these reckless words spread like wildfire on a windy day, and they can't be taken back. Once they are said, they can't be unsaid. Instead, they are repeated and embellished and passed on by those who are gossip-obsessed. Words matter, and words can hurt. Solomon said, "The words of a whisperer are like delicious morsels" (Prov 26:22).

Paul said to stop fighting over words. Such arguments are useless. We should avoid godless, foolish discussions (see 2 Tim 2:14, 16–17).

Jesus said, "On the day of judgment you will have to give an account for every careless word you utter" (Matt 12:36).

As Christians we should pray with the psalmist, "Let the words of my mouth and the meditation of my heart be acceptable to you, O LORD" (Ps 19:14).

Part 3:

Thinking About Religious Beliefs

All Things Work Together

A teenager complained, "Grandma, nothing is working in my life!"

"What do you mean?" she asked.

The boy explained, "You know. At school, at home, my friends, my girlfriend. You know!"

Surprisingly, the wise old woman changed the subject, saying, "Would you like some of this cake I'm making?"

"Sure!" he replied.

"Here! Have a cup of cooking oil."

"Yuck! I can't drink that!"

"How about a couple raw eggs?"

"Gross, Grandma!"

"Would you like some flour?"

"Come on, Grandma. You're making me sick! I want some cake!"

"That's right," his grandmother said. "Each one of these ingredients by itself seems to be bad, but when you put them all together and bake them, they make a great cake."

This is how God works in our lives. Each problem and difficulty taken by itself may seem bad, but the scripture says, "All things work together for good for those who love God" (Rom 8:28).

Bargaining with God

Almost everybody bargains with God. In emergencies we say, "Oh, God, if you'll only do this for me, I'll do this and this and this for you!" We're like the two fellows, lost at sea. One kneels in the raft and prays, "Please, Lord, save us, and we'll go to church, tithe, quit gambling." The other yells, "Hey, wait a minute! Don't promise anything else. I think I see a ship."

Such bargaining is understandable but immature. We don't realize the implications. Omnipotence without omniscience would be a curse! Absolute power without absolute wisdom and absolute love would be deadly!

Suppose you had the ability to really bargain with God. What would you be willing to sacrifice to win the lottery, close that great business deal, or satisfy some deep desire? If your child were in an accident, wouldn't you trade another young person's life to save his? If you had a terminal illness, wouldn't you annihilate faceless people in Romania to get well? Of course all of us would. We're human beings. We are selfish by nature. We have a survival instinct that overrides altruism. We'd wreck the universe to get our own way.

Furthermore, such omnipotence would put us in a catch-22. If we could save our loved ones and didn't, we'd die of guilt. But if we could save our loved ones and did at the expense of someone else, we'd also die of guilt. That's why we can't be omnipotent until we are also omniscient, with full knowledge of consequences. We can't bargain with God until we are totally spiritual beings without earthly egos.

Bargaining sounds good, but it entails awesome responsibilities that we are not ready to handle.

Job realized this when he said, "I have uttered what I did not understand, things too wonderful for me that I did not know" (Job 42:3).

Being Accepted by God

As we mature, we can't jump from A to Z. Instead, we must move one step at a time. That's why the sacrificial rituals and atonement theories that were developed and practiced over the years may have been important and helpful for primitive people. That's why ceremonies such as kneeling at altars, lighting candles, counting beads, being baptized, and observing Communion have become essential elements in many seekers' lives. Even today, we must realize that doing whatever our own particular background has included and our own traditions have taught us may be absolutely necessary to make us feel forgiven and secure.

So if we really need to repeat certain words, then we should say them! If we really need to perform certain procedures, then we should do them! But we shouldn't claim that it's God who requires these observances, and we shouldn't demand that everyone else must do them also to be accepted.

Paul expressed this when he said, "I have lived my life with a clear conscience before God" (Acts 23:1).

That's what God requires from each of us!

Beliefs and Actions

When we believe one way and act another way, we experience stress. Paul said, "I do not understand my own actions. For I do not do what I want, but I do the very thing I hate" (Rom 7:15).

Such cognitive dissonance is unpleasant. Paul summed it up, saying, "Wretched person that I am! Who will rescue me from me from this body of death?" (Rom 7:24).

Since we are uncomfortable, we usually try to reduce the stress. There are several ways to do that. We may deny our feelings, forget the facts, and claim there is no dissonance. If this doesn't work, we may change our belief to match our actions by justifying the deed and calling a vice a virtue.

A few of us may actually do the right thing by changing our actions to match our beliefs. This involves correcting the mistake and resolving not to repeat it.

Ironically, people with low self-esteem experience very little dissonance when they sin. That's because committing an immoral or unsuccessful act is not at odds with their self-concept. If I'm bad, then doing a bad thing seems reasonable.

On the other hand, people with high self-esteem experience great dissonance when they sin. If I believe I'm good, then doing a bad thing seems wrong. That's why our self-concept is so important. It influences our conscience and determines our behavior. If I believe I'm kind, then an unkind action causes dissonance. If I believe I'm smart, then an ignorant action causes dissonance. If I believe I'm frugal, then a wasteful action causes dissonance. If I believe I'm successful, then an unsuccessful action causes dissonance.

If we're unhappy, the reason may be that our beliefs and actions are not in sync. To be happy we must have consonance. That means our beliefs and our actions must match.

Change

Jeremiah describes the difficulty of change by asking, "Can Cushites change their skin or leopards their spots? Then also you can do good, who are accustomed to do evil" (Jer 13:23).

Yes, change is possible, but it's far from easy. In fact, change puts more stress on an organism than anything else. Change is difficult because we become conditioned to certain situations. We get familiar with certain ideas. We grow accustomed to certain habits. Then, unless something traumatic happens to force a change, the law of inertia takes over, and we continue to operate as usual.

Very few people change voluntarily. Jesus said, "The gate is narrow and the road is hard that leads to life, and there are few who find it" (Matt 7:14).

Those courageous few who are willing to change must take three steps:

1. We must use our intellect to determine how the undesirable attitude or behavior began. We must analyze its causes and understand why it occurs. We must discover what current persons, places, or events trigger it.

2. Knowing intellectually that a reaction is unproductive doesn't necessarily eliminate it. We must describe our feelings and name them as precisely as we can. Then we must express our concerns clearly and honestly to a caring person.

Since most feelings are at the subconscious level, they must be expressed several times until their power over us has been broken.

3. Again, knowing something intellectually and feeling something emotionally doesn't necessarily change it. We must deliberately avoid the undesirable behavior and substitute new actions for those that need to be deleted. Every time we refrain from the old, negative response and replace it with the new, positive response, we strengthen the desired behavior. After about twelve times, the old is sublimated, and the new becomes automatic. Isaiah said, "Cease to do evil; learn to do good" (Isa 1:16–17).

Yes, change is hard, but Jesus said, "For God all things are possible" (Matt 19:26).

Computer Morality

A good computer is brilliant, but it's also stupid! It can do fantastic things as long as the data is perfect, the information is exact, and the choices are absolute. It is logical and precise, but it has no flexibility or creativity. It can't make allowances for specific situations or adapt to changing circumstances

Laws are like that. They can achieve order and productivity as long as the issues are clear-cut, the actions are definite, and the decisions are between good and evil, but they have no flexibility or creativity. They can't make allowances for specific situations or adapt to changing circumstances. That's why we must have trials, juries, judges, and updated legislation.

The Pharisees were computers. They had rules for everything. All actions had to be labeled right or wrong, good or bad, legal or illegal. Unfortunately, this didn't work. It hurt people. It caused unnecessary suffering, and it increased misery and guilt.

Jesus wasn't a computer or a legalist. He made allowances for Sabbath-day regulations. He took human needs into consideration, and he adapted religious ceremonies to fit a changing world.

Unfortunately, some Christians seem to have learned nothing from his teachings. Today, we're still operating in computer mode. We're still getting hung up on the creeds and rules and formulas he tried to surpass.

We forget that Jesus stressed freedom, saying, "If the Son makes you free, you will be free indeed" (John 8:36).

Creedal Requirements

Why are we so much stricter in our belief requirements than Jesus was? He never asked his disciples to sign a creedal statement of faith. He never questioned their theology when he asked them to follow him. In fact, he seemed rather unconcerned about what each person believed.

Over and over again, he healed, taught, accepted, and praised those from diverse belief systems without trying to ensure their orthodoxy: "Now the woman was a gentile, of Syrophoenician origin. She begged him to cast the demon out of her daughter. He said to her, 'Let the children be fed first, for it is not fair to take the children's food and throw it to the dogs.' But she answered him, 'Sir, even the dogs under the table eat the children's crumbs.' Then he said to her, 'For saying that, you may go—the demon has left your daughter'" (Mark 7:26–29). Now, why didn't he try to convert this lady to the "right" religion?

He even praised one man from another "faith":

> A centurion came to him, appealing to him and saying, "Lord, my servant is lying at home paralyzed, in terrible distress." And he said to him, "I will come and cure him." The centurion answered, "Lord, I am not worthy to have you come under my roof, but only speak the word, and my servant will be healed. For I also am a man under authority, with soldiers under me, and I say to one, 'Go,' and he goes, and to another, 'Come,' and he comes, and to my slave, 'Do this,' and the slave does it." When Jesus heard him, he was amazed and said to those who followed him, "Truly I tell you, in no one in Israel have I found such faith. I tell you, many will come from east and west and will take their places at the banquet with Abraham and Isaac and Jacob in the kingdom of heaven, while the heirs of the kingdom will be thrown into the outer darkness, where there will be weeping and gnashing of teeth." And Jesus said to the centurion, "Go; let it be done for you according to your faith." (Matt 8:5–13)

The Samaritan he called a "good neighbor" actually believed and practiced what most Jews considered to be downright heresy. But Jesus realized this man's concern and compassion were much more important to God than his position on certain doctrinal matters.

Jesus had no belief requirements because he knew that asking the right questions is much more profound than having all the right answers!

Disturbing Scriptures

It's easy to say, "Love your friends, and hate your enemies." It's even easy to do that. But a disturbing scripture says, "Love your enemies." It also says, "Bless those who curse you; pray for those who mistreat you" (Luke 6:28).

That's not fair! What about the guy who lied to your boss and got you fired? What about that arrogant fellow who cursed you when you invited him to church? What about that old woman who slapped your baby at a daycare center? Surely these are exceptions! But Jesus loved sinners and even prayed for his executioners.

It's easy to "do unto others as they do unto you" and wreak vengeance on evildoers. But a disturbing scripture says, "If you do not forgive others, neither will your Father forgive your trespasses" (Matt 6:15).

That's not fair! Furthermore, must we really do it seventy-seven times?

What about those gangsters who mugged you? What about the drug dealer who got your teen hooked on meth? What about that blonde who seduced your husband and destroyed your marriage? Surely these are exceptions! But Jesus even forgave those soldiers who crucified him.

It's easy to care for and help your family and nice neighbors, but a disturbing scripture says, "Anyone, then, who knows the right thing to do and fails to do it commits sin" (Jas 4:17).

But why should I give my hard-earned money to a lazy beggar? Why should I eat mac and cheese instead of steak to pay for a rebellious young person to go to church camp? Why should I forego my hoped-for vacation to buy Christmas gifts for ungrateful foster children?

That's not fair! But Jesus reminds us that "God sends the blessing of sun and rain on those who don't deserve them."

Yes, there are some disturbing scriptures in the Bible, and following Jesus's commands and example is not always easy!

The Divine/Human Experiment

"The Sabbath was made for humankind and not humankind for the Sabbath" (Mark 2:27). This mind-blowing idea distinguishes our faith from all other religions. Jesus broke the rules that didn't serve human beings and promoted the precepts that did. He told us that as mature sons and daughters of God, we have access to all the resources of God.

There are no forbidden areas or unknowable answers! The rending of the veil in the temple dramatically symbolized the fact that nothing is off limits to us! We have a right to approach the divine province with questions and problems. Jesus said, "I do not call you servants any longer, because the servant does not know what the master is doing, but I have called you friends, because I have made known to you everything that I have heard from my Father" (John 15:15).

As mature sons and daughters of God, we also share the responsibilities of God. Let's imagine that an astronaut is trained and sent up in a space capsule. Suppose he folds his hands and says, "I'll just be submissive, and I'm sure ground control will take me where they want me to go!" What nonsense! He's in control. To the extent that the pilot is willing to listen to instructions and follow through on the information, he will succeed. If he refuses to learn and act, he will fail!

Now, if the vehicle had been set on automatic pilot, preprogrammed to follow a certain course, or if it had been designed as a remote-control experiment to be operated by experts back in the space center, then the pilot would have been unnecessary. Instead, this mission was planned as a joint project; therefore, ground control can't do it without him!

Life is like that. This universe has not been set on autopilot. It has not been preprogrammed to follow a certain course. It is not being operated by remote control. It's a joint project—a divine/human experiment. God can't do it without us!

Don't Check Your Brain at the Door

The most self-defeating thing Christianity has done is to promote the ridiculous notion that believers should check their brains at the door of the church.

God created brains! Thinking is not a sin! Questioning is not a sin! Doubting is not a sin! Throughout biblical history there have always been those rare individuals who dared to rise above the status quo. These sincere, deep-minded thinkers simply refused to accept every current teaching—even those considered sacred and inspired. We often forget that prophets like Jeremiah, Hosea, and Amos rejected many of the pervading doctrines and belief systems of their time and were persecuted for their "heresy."

Then, surprisingly, Jesus himself became the ultimate changemaker. Few readers realize the significance of the following statement: "You have heard that it was said, 'An eye for an eye and a tooth for a tooth.' But I say to you: Do not resist an evildoer" (Matt 5:38–39).

According to Old Testament scriptures, those words he so casually repudiated were claimed to be a direct command from God (see Lev 24:1, 20, 23). Over and over, Jesus was accused of dishonoring God and destroying religion (see Matt 9:3).

                                           Think (Or Else!)

Again, today, we're facing a serious crisis. The message of truth is not reaching this generation. Insisting upon presenting the same old precepts in updated language won't work. Jesus expected growth and development. He envisioned a living faith. In fact, he said, "I still have many things to say to you, but you cannot bear them now" (John 16:12).

What are those unexpressed things? And when will we be ready to deal with them? Well, that time has come! As Christians who live in a world with more information and greater understanding than ever before, it's our responsibility to discover and share these important insights! To do that we must not check our brains at the door. Instead, we must bring them with us into our faith situations. We must use our logical abilities. We must think!

Do You Know Jesus?

When someone asks, "Do you know Jesus?" Christians usually say, "Sure, I know Jesus!" But do we *really* know Jesus?

Knowing a few things about him is not enough. Marveling at his miraculous deeds is not enough. Many of us fail to realize that we're commanded to follow Jesus, to be like Jesus, to carry out Jesus's message and ministry. To do this, we desperately need to know as many details as possible about his humanity.

We can't duplicate Jesus's godly powers, but we can and must duplicate his human qualities. We must know how he felt, how he thought, what he said, and what he did. We must examine his purposes, his attitudes, and his character traits.

Many ideas people have about Jesus are stereotypes. They are not based on the scriptures. He wasn't merely a religious icon. He certainly wasn't a pious fanatic. Instead, he was an interesting and vital individual. He expressed strong feelings of impatience, anger, and depression, as well as joy, sympathy, and love. He was a logical thinker. His teachings and stories emphasized concern for others and hatred for hypocrisy and greed. He was a man with a lot of common sense and humor.

To really know Jesus we must develop an understanding of his personality. We must come to know him as a friend as well as a savior. Unfortunately, very little research of this nature is available, and very few churches deal with these issues.

Understanding Jesus's activities and achievements will help us know him better and become more like him. That's important, because the scripture says, "Whoever says, 'I abide in him,' ought to walk in the same way as he walked" (1 John 2:6).

Dumbo's Feather

In a delightful little tale, an elephant named Dumbo wants to fly. Some friendly birds give him lessons, plus a blue feather from the best flyer's wing. Dumbo believes that as long as he carries the "magic" feather, he cannot fall. All goes well at first, and Dumbo performs great feats before huge audiences. Then one day, in a panic, he discovers that he has dropped his feather. As soon as he notices his loss, he begins to plummet. All at once, he remembers he had been flying without the feather until he realized it was gone. At that moment he understands that the miracle of flight is not in the feather, but in his own ability, plus his belief in the feather.

So where do miracles come from?

First, there is faith in ourselves. We must have self-respect and self-confidence. We must trust our instincts and value our strengths.

Second, there is faith in others. We must rely on our support group. We must abolish cynicism and expect the best from those around us.

Third, there is faith in universal principles. We must have a positive attitude. We must believe that life is ultimately on the side of truth and righteousness.

Fourth, there is faith in God. We must worship a just and loving creator instead of a vindictive deity.

Feathers can't make us fly, but faith can!

Paul said, "We walk by faith" (2 Cor 5:7).

Gnats or Camels?

Jesus said, "You strain out a gnat but swallow a camel!" (Matt 23:24).

Why do Christian groups constantly engage in "anti-gnat" crusades? Jesus wasted absolutely no time on trivial matters. He never criticized anyone's dress or lack thereof. He ignored what people ate and drank. He didn't lead any protest movements. He didn't stage any demonstrations. He didn't boycott any businesses.

Why? Wasn't there any sin in those days? Weren't there any prostitutes in Jerusalem? Wasn't there any pornography? Weren't there any pagan practices? Of course there were, but he knew you can never reform the world by stamping out the evil. You can only change the world by strengthening the good. Jesus chose to deal with internal causes rather than external symptoms. He said, "First clean the inside of the cup and of the plate, so that the outside also may become clean" (Matt 23:26).

Jesus warned against the sins of hypocrisy, unconcern, and greed (see Matt 23:23, 25). Today, there are few crusades against these things!

In fact, the only people Jesus really condemned were the law-abiding, self-righteous religious leaders—the ones who were very much like the leaders of the "anti-gnat" movements today.

"God Don't Make Beds!"

Two children stood looking out the window at an arch of colors in the mist. Suddenly, the older boy made a smug pronouncement: "God makes rainbows! God makes everything!"

"Well," his little brother replied, with a sad glance at their messy, disorganized room, "God sure don't make beds!"

This casual observation expresses a deep theological puzzle. Why does God make rainbows but not beds? Why does God make mountains but not skyscrapers? Why does God make oceans but not bathtubs? What is creation? Where does the divine aspect stop and the human aspect start? What differentiates raw material from finished products? What's the heavenly part, and what's the earthly part?

Understanding this simple question would help us deal with the issue of supernatural miracles and answers to prayer.

As honest observers, we must admit that while there is ample evidence that God provides natural resources, there is almost no reliable evidence that he ever refines them. He set up the process that caused manna to form, but he didn't gather it or grind it or bake it (see Num 11:2, 8). He made iron ore, but he never made a needle!

Once, an old frontier preacher was being heckled by an obnoxious drunk. The fellow stood on a stump and yelled, "If God is real, tell him to knock me off of this stump right now!"

After enduring a few minutes of this, the preacher calmly laid down his Bible, walked over to the heckler, and laid him out! The crowd froze in astonishment as the preacher looked down at the drunk and said, "I never ask the Lord to do anything I can handle by myself."

You see, we can't create worlds and universes and natural resources, but we can make beds. It's obvious that God's part stops where ours begins!

God Sees the Big Picture

A man in a small business aircraft was flying over some rugged terrain when he saw an automobile trying to pass a large truck. He said it was obvious that the driver of the car was impatient to get around the truck. He kept crossing back and forth from one lane to the other. But each time the driver tried to pass, he would either reach a double line, a hill, a curve, or another car. The pilot, who could see several miles down the highway, thought, "If I could just talk with that man in the automobile, I could tell him when it is safe to pass and when it is unsafe."

That's the story of God and man. Our vision is limited. God is omniscient. He sees the big picture.

Job says that God "sees everything under the heavens" (Job 28:24).

God's Tough Love

The scripture says, "God is love" (1 John 4:8).

That's true! Nothing is more certain than that. However, what does this love entail? What kind of love does God exemplify?

We've all heard of God's compassion, of God's mercy, of God's forgiveness, of God's grace. But there's another side to God's love. What about God's "tough love"? Both Jesus and Paul emphasize this principle.

First, Jesus advises us against continuing to deal with those who are obviously unresponsive and close-minded. He said, "If anyone will not welcome you or listen to your words, shake off the dust from your feet as you leave that house or town" (Matt 10:14).

Next, Jesus warns us to avoid wasting our efforts with those who are arrogant and unconcerned. He said, "Do not give what is holy to dogs, and do not throw your pearls before swine, or they will trample them under foot and turn and maul you" (Matt 7:6).

Finally, Paul gives us an adamant and almost ruthless rule about permanently supporting those who are lazy and irresponsible. He said, "Anyone unwilling to work should not eat" (2 Thess 3:10).

There are no biblical admonitions that require us to become naive and gullible "do-gooders." God doesn't want us to enable unproductive and dangerous behavior by encouraging apathy and indolence. Instead, he wants us to spend our time and resources ministering to those who respond and make honest efforts in their own behalf. Remember, the servant who did nothing with his talent was punished, not rewarded.

Jesus explained God's "tough love" when he said, "To all those who have, more will be given, and they will have an abundance, but from those who have nothing, even what they have will be taken away" (Matt 25:29).

How Free Are We?

When Jesus said, "You are free," he meant it! Unlike so many religious leaders today, he never pressured a person to respond to his call. He never pressured a follower to remain in his movement. In fact, he did the very opposite. He urged people to stop and think. He advised people to count the cost.

"Free! Free! Free!" runs like an overriding theme throughout the scriptures. Adam and Eve were free to eat. There were no bars around the forbidden fruit. Cain was free to kill. There were no guards to protect Abel. Joseph was free to boast. Lot's wife was free to look back. David was free to commit adultery. The rich young ruler was free to walk away. Judas was free to betray Jesus.

We are free to accept or reject God's call. Paul said, "Christ has set us free. Stand firm, therefore, and do not submit again to a yoke of slavery" (Gal 5:1).

Jesus in the Twenty-First Century

Could we accept Jesus as a twenty-first century personality? Basic problems never change. There are always human needs, social tensions, and superficial religions, but archaic terms and obsolete conditions tend to dull the impact of the gospel. If our lives are to be affected, we must have the courage to get him out of white robes, take him off the donkey, and let him speak to us.

Indeed, if Jesus came today, he probably wouldn't even be considered religious! He was simply too lax on piety! He socialized with undesirable characters (see Matt 11:18–19). He ignored orthodox rules (see Matt 12:1–2). He alienated the influential and elevated children and women above preachers and leaders (see Matt 21:31; 23:13; Luke 18:17; 21:1–4). In short, he a troublemaker and a nonconformist!

Taken seriously, Christianity would revolutionize this world! Millions of people, especially the young, who are turned off by our institutional religion could become enthusiastically turned on to our Christ. Few have dared explore Jesus's distinctive lifestyle. Cultural conditioning has blurred the original. The artificial formulas and phrases that so monopolize evangelical attention are a far cry from the life-affirming concepts announced by the Master!

Going back to the "old-time religion" means going all the way back—past Victorian prudery, past Reformation fanaticism, and even past Paul's systematized applications. If we persist, we'll finally unveil a man who superseded rules, despised creeds, and refused to define morality codes. He lived freely, abundantly, and productively. And that's the way he wants us to live!

Jesus spent more time on psychological principles than he did on theological doctrines! If we take an honest look at his ministry, we'll find that he totally ignored all those things denominations fight about today. He wasted no energy condemning pornography or outlawing prostitution! He gave no doctrinal tests. Instead, he talked about attitudes, motives, and practical social relationships.

Examining Jesus's gospel shows that our emphases are often exactly opposite to his! Too often, we've majored on minors and minored on majors! An intense study of Jesus's parables and teachings can change our lives!

Lack of Knowledge

Years ago, God said, "My people are destroyed for lack of knowledge!" (Hos 4:6).

Even though information in science and technology is increasing so rapidly that it's hard to keep up, people today are still being destroyed for lack of knowledge.

When Solomon was granted one wish, he asked for wisdom. God was pleased and added other blessings, saying, "Wisdom and knowledge are granted to you. I will also give you riches, possessions, and honor" (2 Chron 1:12).

This always happens. People want happiness, success, and financial security. In fact, they may spend their lives seeking these things and never find them. But when we get knowledge, it brings with it happiness, success, and financial security. With all the books, universities, internet information, and educational programs available today, there is no excuse for being ill-informed.

Christianity desperately needs knowledge and thinkers who use it. So much ignorance is labeled as "moral concern."

Once, a school was dealing with controversial material. When a student told his mother about his lessons, she immediately called her pastor and began alerting other parents.

At the next school board meeting there was a packed house. One by one, people stepped up to the microphone to give highly emotional tirades against the curriculum. When the meeting reached a feverish pitch, the board asked for a show of hands from the individuals who had actually read the material. There were only five! Immediately, the crowd lost its credibility.

Too many discussions and crusades are just a pooling of ignorance. We need to do our homework. The only opinions that are worthwhile are informed opinions.

If Christianity is to influence the modern world, it must be rooted in reality. It must have factual data. It must not deal in superstitions. It must not emphasize the sentimental and emotional aspects of religion while it neglects the practical and sensible aspects.

James said, "If any of you is lacking in wisdom, ask God, who gives to all generously and ungrudgingly, and it will be given you" (Jas 1:5).

The Letter Kills

Paul explained that the new covenant was not of the letter but of the Spirit. He said, "The letter kills, but the Spirit gives life" (2 Cor 3:6).

When Paul says the letter kills, he is telling us that our beliefs and actions must not be based upon old writings but upon a new Spirit. He said, "We are enslaved in the newness of the Spirit and not in the oldness of the written code" (Rom 7:6).

Saying the Spirit must take precedence proves that Paul did not expect his own words to become legal requirements. He never claimed inerrancy. He even said, "I see through a glass darkly." Yet, today, such an opinion would be highly controversial. An insinuation that anything supersedes the "inerrant, infallible, written scripture" would be instantly condemned!

Now, Paul isn't repudiating all scripture (see 2 Tim 3:15). Instead, he is reminding us that the same writings can be used to kill or to give life.

If we come to scriptures with preconceived notions, if we use them in a legalistic way, if we stifle our own spiritual intuitions to follow the letter of the Law, or if we use these writings to criticize, condemn, or control others, then it kills! It kills our own growth, and it kills productive social relationships.

On the other hand, if we bring our intellect to the scriptures, if we filter all isolated verses through the mind of Christ, if we let the Holy Spirit apply its interpretation, then it can give life.

Paul felt obligated to voice these warnings because truth is in God, not in written words! This is obvious because Satan himself quoted scriptures, and there is no truth in him (see Matt 4:6; John 8:44).

Truth can only reside in us when the Holy Spirit of God is in us. Jesus said, "He will give you another Advocate, to be with you forever. This is the Spirit of truth…. When the Spirit of truth comes, he will guide you into all the truth" (John 14:16–17; 16:13).

That's why Paul says the letter of the Law, which consists of isolated written words and phrases and commandments, can kill, but the Spirit, which is the divine presence in our rational soul, gives life!

Liberty

When the movie *Jonathan Livingston Seagull* was being filmed, the gulls looked like they had total freedom of movement. Actually, they were tied to their perches with almost invisible strings. People are like that. Many individuals seem to be rich, famous, and happy. In fact, they are tied by strings of guilt, fear, and resentment. These almost invisible fetters cause the problems in our lives.

All normal people want to make their own choices and realize their own dreams. This is a God-given right. Individuals who feel restrained will eventually become bitter and depressed.

Unfortunately, many religions have added even more constraints with rules and moral demands. The Jews calculated the exact number of steps a person could take on the Sabbath without sinning. They debated whether eating an egg that was laid on the Sabbath was a sin. Jesus was criticized for healing a person on the Sabbath.

Christianity has its own moral dilemmas. A generation ago, dancing was considered a sin, but if you had wheels on your feet, the same action was called skating, and that wasn't a sin. Some churches divide and argue over gender issues, lifestyle choices, and even political parties. Rules are terrible taskmasters.

Surprisingly, many people avoid autonomy. They want to be told exactly what to do. But Jesus broke laws to help people! He said, "If the Son makes you free, you will be free indeed" (John 8:36). He never forced anyone to do his will. He called the rich young ruler. He loved the rich young ruler, but he allowed him to walk away. Jesus yearned for the people of Jerusalem to respond to his message, but he let them make bad choices (see Matt 23:37).

Many pious individuals seek authoritarian leaders. They want superheroes! They want reassurance that someone has the answers to life's questions. They may join legalistic cults or vote for dictatorial politicians.

Too many of us obey mindless creeds and follow the crowd. In fact, we do everything but believe in ourselves. Yet the gospel promises that our answers are deep within us. The poet Edgar A. Guest wrote:

> The power to choose the work we do,
> To grow and have a larger view,
> To not submit to king or state,

To be the master of our fate,
To know, to feel that we are free—
That is called autonomy!

True Christianity encourages autonomy. The Holy Spirit is our internal guidance system. God gave each of us a unique personality and a unique purpose. Our Christian walk will look different from everyone else's, and that's okay!

Life or Religion?

Is God as interested in giraffes as he is in angels? Is God as concerned about laboratories as he is about cathedrals? Is God as disturbed about pollution as he is promiscuity?

These questions may seem ludicrous to traditional Christians. It never occurs to us that God is interested in animal husbandry even though he created living things and gave us dominion over them: "Subdue it and have dominion over… every living thing that moves upon the earth" (Gen 1:28).

It never occurs to us that God is concerned with genetic research even though he created human beings and commissioned to be productive: "Be fruitful and multiply and fill the earth" (Gen 1:28).

It never occurs to us that God is disturbed about soil erosion even though he created the earth and the herbs and told us to use them well: "I have given you every plant yielding seed…and every tree with seed in its fruit; you shall have them for food" (Gen 1:29).

We've so separated God from his universe that we don't even think of him as a brilliant creator. We think of him as a petty moralist. This attitude is neither scriptural nor reasonable.

In the beginning God spent the vast majority of his time and effort on this natural world (see Gen 1:5–23). Furthermore, God was pleased with his work: "God saw everything that he had made, and indeed, it was very good" (Gen 1:31). Therefore, why wouldn't he be as interested and concerned and disturbed about our behavior in the areas of astronomy, geology, and biology as he is about our behavior in the area of religion?

In fact, this is a unified universe. Either all of it is of God or none of it is of God! God inspires scientists working with test tubes as surely as he inspires preachers working with sermons. God calls physicists to analyze chemistry and nuclear elements as surely as he calls theologians to analyze Greek and Hebrew texts. God guides the anthropologist as surely as he guides the missionary.

Yes, God is interested in giraffes and laboratories and pollution. The scriptures tell of a God who made a natural universe, not a supernatural institution. The scriptures tell of a Son of God who gives us a more abundant life, not a more complicated religion.

A "New Testament Church"

Many people insist we must be a "New Testament church," but there's no such thing! Trying to do everything like the apostles did is both impossible and unreasonable. They had no sound systems, no hymnals, no pews, no air conditioning, and no buildings. They certainly didn't have family centers and buses for transportation.

Some say since Paul told women to be silent in one first-century situation, that commandment is still universally operative today. But another passage tells slaves to obey their masters (see Col 3:22), and we say, "Oh, that's not applicable now." What's the difference?

Also, New Testament members sold their property and gave the proceeds to the poor (see Acts 4:34–35), but few modern-day legalists do that! In fact, it's biblical to elect deacons by "rolling the dice" (see Acts 1:26), but no church follows that example. Must we turn all our books into scrolls in order to be a "New Testament church"?

You see, life progresses. Cultural change is inevitable, and if we make transient customs into absolute laws, then we are doing exactly what the Pharisees did—"quenching the Spirit." Jesus didn't insist on obeying "Mt. Sinai" rules and using "Mt. Sinai" methods. Instead, he advocated putting new wine in new bottles (see Matt 9:17).

Jesus went far beyond the past customs and changed obsolete rules, and so must we! Adapting to modern life is not being sinful! Paul said, "I have become all things to all people, that I might by all means save some" (1 Cor 9:22).

Of Rules and Sins

Breaking a rule is not necessarily committing a sin. Jesus broke many rules. The scriptures give a very strict rule about working on the Sabbath. This rule is even one of the Ten Commandments. But Jesus said there are other things that are more important. If a person is hurting, you should break the rule and help them. Even if an animal is in need, you should break the rule and alleviate its distress (see Luke 13:14–16; 14:5).

Jesus supported his disciples when they broke the rule by gathering grain on the Sabbath (see Matt 12:1–5). He also reminded his critics that there was a rule about not entering a sacred area of the tabernacle and eating special bread. Yet David and his men broke that rule when they were hungry (see Matt 12:3–5).

Jesus was constantly being attacked and criticized for breaking rules. He ate with sinners. He touched lepers. He forgave adulterers. He defended prostitutes. He discussed religion with women. He surprised everyone by praising Mary for her intellectual and spiritual interests rather than Martha for her domestic skills (see Luke 10:40–42).

Jesus talked more about the inward sins of the heart—such as hate, lust, and covetousness—than he did about the outward sins that break rules—such as murder, adultery, and theft (see Matt 23:23, 27). He said many rules are just "gnats" (see Matt 23:14).

So breaking a rule is not necessarily committing a sin. In fact, sometimes not breaking a rule in order to achieve a higher good is the sin!

One Important Word

Jesus's final message says, "Go…and make disciples of all nations…teaching them to obey everything that I have commanded you" (Matt 28:19–20).

All of us have heard this great commission, but we may have missed the most important word: He said, "Teach them what *I* have told you," not what Moses taught you, not what Paul is going to teach you, and not what some religious group may choose to teach you.

In other words, if you can't find where the Lord himself teaches something about a particular moral principle, you should probably leave it alone!

Only God Knows

Only God knows the value of the hidden talents and possibilities within each person. For years, tourists visiting the Capitol in Washington, D.C., have stopped to marvel at one of Gutzon Borglum's best-known sculptures, a huge head of Lincoln. When Borglum was working on this piece of art, his concentration was interrupted by a family who came to visit his studio. The face was just beginning to emerge on one side of the enormous stone.

The five-year-old daughter of the couple stood before the granite block and gazed in wonder at the giant features of Lincoln's face. After a few minutes of contemplation, the little girl ran over to Borglum and tugged at his sleeve. "Mister," she said, "is that Abraham Lincoln?"

"Yes! Yes, it is!" he replied.

"Well," the little girl queried, "I just want to know one thing. How did you know he was in there?"

We don't always know what's "in there." When we meet someone and make a judgment based on a first impression, it's often superficial. Fortunately, Jesus always saw the value that was in people. He said, "You are of more value than many sparrows" (Matt 10:31).

Our World Needs Heroes

Our world today needs heroes! But who is a hero? A hero is not a perfect person, because there are none. Instead, the word *hero* means, "an individual whose higher aspirations are able to overcome his lower instincts."

We are all mixtures of good and bad. When Thomas Jefferson wrote in the Declaration of Independence that "all men are created equal," he owned over one hundred slaves and saw no contradiction.

Once, a man asked Jesus to heal his son. Jesus told him, "All things are possible to those who believe." The man replied, "I believe; help my unbelief!" (Mark 9:24).

Well, all of us believe, but we also doubt. All of us love, but we also hate. All of us are concerned, but we are also unconcerned. All of us have both negative and positive elements in our character. Rahab was a prostitute and a brothel madam, yet she was blessed as an ancestor of Jesus. David was an adulterer and a murderer, yet he was "a man after God's own heart." Paul encouraged the stoning of Stephen and persecuted the church, yet he wrote much of the New Testament.

You see, God can use imperfect people. A wise man said, "Even broken trees can bear sweet fruit."

One of Jesus's greatest insights was the realization that individuals with "minor sins" (pride, greed, and self-righteousness) probably hurt more people than individuals with "major sins" (theft, sexual immorality). That's why he said, "The tax collectors and the prostitutes are going into the kingdom of God ahead of you" (Matt 21:31).

So don't claim perfection. Instead, recognize and admit your own weaknesses and shortcomings. Let your higher aspirations overcome your lower instincts, and you will be a hero!

The Religion of Jesus

As Christians do we proclaim the principles Jesus actually taught and lived by, or do we proclaim the principles other people have told us about Jesus? It's obvious that much of our "gospel" is not based on the teachings of Jesus himself.

Jesus emphasized basic life skills. He advocated personal discipline, good relationships, and the productive use of talents and resources. These things are so ordinary that we don't often even associate them with religion. Yet they are desperately needed in our world today.

Jesus was practical. He ridiculed many of the elaborate rituals being practiced in his day. He said, "The Sabbath was made for man." Therefore, "If an ox falls in a ditch, pull him out."

He said, "Worship must consist of giving cups of cold water, and reconciling social conflicts, as well as prayers and hymns." He even gave surprising advice concerning his own ministry when he said, "If I am not doing the works of my Father, then do not believe me" (John 10:37).

Contrary to a popular stereotype, Jesus was not a religious fanatic. Instead, he led a balanced life and was criticized for it. He said, "You can't please everybody": "John came neither eating nor drinking, and they say, 'He has a demon'; the Son of Man came eating and drinking, and they say, 'Look, a glutton and a drunkard, a friend of tax collectors and sinners!'" (Matt 11:18–19).

Jesus associated with the wrong crowd. People complained to his followers, saying, "Why does your teacher eat with tax collectors and sinners?" (Matt 9:11).

Jesus broke religious laws. The leaders were indignant because Jesus healed a woman on the Sabbath. They said, "There are six days on which work ought to be done; come on those days and be cured and not on the Sabbath day" (Luke 13:14).

Jesus compromised with regulations and paid taxes even though he didn't agree with the government policies, saying, "Give therefore to Caesar the things that are the emperor's, and to God the things that are God's" (Matt 22:21).

Jesus evaluated the importance of things differently from most moralists and said, "Woe to you, scribes and Pharisees, hypocrites! For you tithe mint, dill, and cumin and have neglected the weightier matters of the law: justice and mercy and faith" (Matt 23:23).

Jesus wasn't out knocking on doors trying to "save souls" twenty-four hours a day. He certainly taught and helped people, but he also rested, interacted with children, attended celebrations, and socialized with friends and acquaintances.

So after more than two thousand years, isn't it time we discovered and began to emphasize the real religion of Jesus?

Religion or Real Life?

Christians have too often separated religion from "real life." They tend to pit the heart against the brain. They emphasize feelings and denigrate thinking. They present piety and practicality as either/or choices. That's a tragic mistake, because Jesus presented his gospel as not only a vital part of life but life at the highest degree. It's life as it was meant to be lived. He said, "I came that they may have life and have it abundantly" (John 10:10).

Jesus never suggested that we must choose between religion and science, or religion and reason, or religion and common sense. Instead, he realized that faith motivates science; faith utilizes reason; faith validates common sense. James said, "Faith by itself, if it has no works, is dead" (Jas 2:17).

Salvation

Evangelicals often describe salvation as something that's achieved through agreeing to a brief formula. But if there is one exact way to move a person from an "unsaved" to a "saved" position, then why didn't Jesus explain that magic procedure to everyone he met?

If going through a quick and easy process can change a sinner into a saint, then why didn't Jesus repeat that process to all his followers?

If a particular "repentance, belief, commitment" routine is required before a soul is converted, then why didn't Jesus make that the core of every lesson he taught and every sermon he preached?

When we honestly examine Jesus's witnessing techniques, we find there is no one formula or process or procedure that guarantees salvation. Instead, Jesus evaluated each individual and expressed his recommendations in ways to meet that person's needs.

To Jesus, salvation is not merely a ticket to heaven. It is the way to attain a rich and abundant life, for now and for eternity. With James and John, he said, "Leave your occupation and follow me." With the woman at the well, he questioned her past problems and said, "Let me quench your thirst with living water." With the rich young ruler, he asked about his moral code and then told him to get rid of his wealth. With one crowd, he insisted they should become "childlike." With Nicodemus, who obeyed all the rules and considered himself morally acceptable, Jesus advised him to be "born again." Jesus counseled Samaritans, Syro-Phoenicians, and Roman centurions without requiring them to immediately abandon their own religious systems and subscribe to a new creed.

Salvation means attaining wholeness. Jesus helped each person reach that state, not to satisfy an angry God but to ensure a successful, productive, abundant life (see John 10:10).

Seeing Values

God's divine presence in us and in others must not be denied, reviled, or treated as worthless! A traveler in the diamond fields of South Africa once saw a boy throwing rocks. When one of them fell at the stranger's feet, he picked it up and was about to return it when an unexpected flash caught his eye! This was a diamond, yet the child was treating it as a common stone.

The peasant's foot had kicked that rock, and the cart wheels had crushed that rock. It had been considered totally worthless until someone recognized its value.

That's our story. How often do we fail to see value in our family and friends? How often do we fail to see value in opportunities we are offered? How often do we fail to see value in spiritual things?

Jesus said, "Do not store up for yourselves treasures on earth, where moth and rust consume and where thieves break in and steal" (Matt 6:19).

Paul said, "Set your minds on the things that are above, not on the things that are on earth" (Col 3:2).

Sell Your Possessions or Be Born Again

The scripture says, "Sell what you own, and give the money to the poor" (Mark 10:21).

The scripture also says, "No one can see the kingdom of God without being born from above" (John 3:3).

Both of these admonitions are in the Bible. Both of these admonitions are direct quotes from Jesus. So how are they different?

The main difference is that one has been ignored and rejected as "not applicable" for us while the other has been used as an absolute universal formula for salvation.

Why is that?

Well, in the episode with the rich young ruler, Jesus was speaking to a particular man in a particular situation. He realized the besetting sin in this man's life was materialism, so he spoke to that. In the episode with Nicodemus, Jesus was also speaking to a particular man in a particular situation. He realized the besetting sin in this man's life was self-righteousness, so he spoke to that.

Orthodox Jews of Jesus's generation felt they were automatically born into God's favor because they were the chosen race. They believed all other races had to be spiritually "reborn" as Jews to be accepted by God. That's the question Jesus was addressing.

Jesus was explaining to Nicodemus that he needed regeneration every bit as much as a gentile. That's how the phrase *new birth* became a symbol of conversion.

Using the phrase to describe salvation is perfectly acceptable if we understand its context and purpose, but it's not acceptable if we use it to repudiate those who choose to describe their spiritual relationships in other ways. A "born again" Christian is no better than a "Jesus following" Christian (see John 4:14), a "child-like" Christian (see Matt 18:3), or a "truth freed" Christian (see John 8:32).

Born again is a metaphor or descriptive illustration, not a magic formula. Those who insist it must be applied literally and universally will have to apply other admonitions from Jesus's mouth, such as "sell what you own," just as literally and universally.

Talents

In the parable of the talents, the master, who represents God, went into a far country. The servants, who represent us, were left to deal with his resources. In this account God didn't manipulate his servants, command his servants, or even advise his servants. Instead, when he put them in charge of his resources, he expected them to be autonomous and independent. He allowed them to think for themselves, to choose their own methods, and to carry out their own actions. In fact, he let them make some decisions that we might call "playing God."

It's strange that the one who was so very conservative and cautious because he feared and reverenced God was the one who was totally condemned. Those who dared to risk by trying new and different business ventures were generously rewarded (see Matt 25:14ff.).

This is not the "life lesson" that is taught by most religions!

Teaching or Preaching

Jesus was practical. He didn't appreciate long prayers, often saying, "When you are praying, do not heap up empty phrases as the gentiles do, for they think that they will be heard because of their many words" (Matt 6:7).

He detested empty, pious platitudes, saying, "Not everyone who says to me, 'Lord, Lord,' will enter the kingdom of heaven, but only the one who does the will of my Father in heaven" (Matt 7:21).

On another occasion he said, "This people honors me with their lips, but their hearts are far from me" (Matt 15:8).

One interesting encounter illustrates his attitude about sanctimonious expressions. As Jesus was talking, "a woman in the crowd raised her voice and said to him, 'Blessed is the womb that bore you and the breast that nursed you!'" Instead of being pleased with her adoration, he replied, "Blessed rather are those who hear the word of God and obey it!" (Luke 11:27–28).

It's unfortunate that some people don't attend church to learn information or receive encouragement. Instead, these individuals feel that church services must involve emotional outbursts and severe threats. Contrary to what many evangelists believe, Jesus never preached "hellfire and damnation" sermons. Now, he did get angry and warn evildoers, but these outbursts were always directed at self-righteous religious hypocrites who judged those around them. He never attacked groups of listeners and seekers. Instead, he grieved over them. The scripture says, "When he saw the crowds, he had compassion for them because they were harassed and helpless, like sheep without a shepherd" (Matt 9:36).

In fact, Jesus seldom "preached" at anyone. Instead, most of the time he just told stories. The scripture says, "With many such parables he spoke the word to them…. He did not speak to them except in parables" (Mark 4:33–34).

His teaching style is emphasized over and over. Mark says, "Crowds again gathered around him, and, as was his custom, he again taught them" (Mark 10:1).

John says, "All the people came to him, and he sat down and began to teach them" (John 8:2).

Jesus said, "Day after day I sat in the temple teaching" (Matt 26:55). You don't calmly sit when you're pounding the pulpit or giving emotional tirades.

Yes, Jesus taught, and that's what he commanded us to do, saying, "Go therefore and make disciples of all nations…teaching them to obey everything that I have commanded you" (Matt 28:19–20).

People need information much more than they need condemnation. They need reasoning ability much more than they need exciting entertainment. They need compassionate teachers much more than they need fanatic orators.

That's Not Fair!

One of the hardest lessons we must learn is that life isn't always fair. We hate to admit that the world doesn't operate equitably, because we're taught from birth that causes and effects are consistent. Even some Old Testament scriptures lead us to believe that life is fair. The psalmist says, "The LORD lifts up the downtrodden; he casts the wicked to the ground" (Ps 147:6).

Solomon says, "One who walks in integrity will be safe, but whoever follows crooked ways will fall into the Pit" (Prov 28:18).

Over and over, we're told that if we do good things, we'll receive good things, and if we do bad things, we'll receive bad things. Unfortunately, that's not always true.

Jesus tries to correct this misinformation. In fact, he says the opposite. If we do good things, we often receive bad things. He said, "They will hand you over to be tortured and will put you to death, and you will be hated by all nations because of my name" (Matt 24:9).

Furthermore, he says God is even-handed. "He makes his sun rise on the evil and on the good and sends rain on the righteous and on the unrighteous" (Matt 5:45).

In fact, the crucifixion stands forever as a symbol of the unfairness of life. The best person received the worst treatment. The innocent Jesus is killed, and the guilty Barabbas goes free. It's not fair!

The gospel doesn't promise fairness in every situation. However, we do have the assurance that, ultimately, right will prevail. Jesus said, "In the world you face persecution, but take courage: I have conquered the world!" (John 16:33).

Three Needs

Someone said, "People need three things: to be fed, to be mystified, and to be controlled."

Jesus's temptations deal with these three issues. Satan, in effect, said, "You're hungry. Make bread from stones, and you'll be fed." Then he said, "You're doing ordinary things. People won't listen to you. Jump off the temple, and you'll have a magical experience, and people will be mystified." Finally, he said, "You're weak and without possessions. Worship me, and I'll be responsible for you and provide for you."

Perhaps these three areas are symbolic of all the temptations of mankind: To be fed means to have our physical needs met with material things. To be mystified means to be intrigued and entertained. To be controlled means to be in a risk-free environment with limited options and limited responsibilities.

A dictator fills all these needs, especially if he has a religious connection or makes supernatural claims. Early Roman rulers knew this when they said, "Give them bread and circuses."

Jesus, on the other hand, refused to fill these three "needs" because he knew that would lead people to enslavement. When the immature crowd wanted to be fed, he said, "One does not live by bread alone" (Luke 4:4).

When they wanted to be mystified, he said, "An evil and adulterous generation asks for a sign, but no sign will be given to it" (Matt 12:39).

When they wanted to be controlled, "Jesus…withdrew again to the mountain by himself" (John 6:15).

Now, these three needs are legitimate, but outside sources can't fill them. As mature individuals we must satisfy our own needs. We must earn our own daily bread, discover our own inner mysteries, and develop our own self-control.

True, False, or Otherwise

We hear a lot today about false doctrine and heresy. For most people false doctrine means your doctrine. For most people, heresy means whatever I disagree with!

Throughout history, great pain has been inflicted in the name of exposing false doctrine, stamping out heresy, and defending religion. The Inquisitions, the burnings at the stake, and the Crusades were all supposedly perpetrated to protect truth. That's nonsense! Truth doesn't need protection. Truth will triumph!

If you really believe in your faith, you won't panic when it's challenged. You won't react violently when people express different views. The future of both democracy and Christianity depends upon their willingness to tolerate and even encourage diversity. If the social system is such that all ideas are allowed free rein, then that which is true will win and that which is false will lose.

Trying to protect against heresy is much more dangerous than heresy itself. The censorship that silences dissent and muffles criticism also screens out new insights. Every invention and discovery of mankind has had to battle the heresy hunters. Every original development and innovation has had to contend with the misguided conservers of the status quo. If civilization had succumbed to the pressure of all the "correct doctrine" advocates, we'd still believe in a flat earth and live in caves.

Why can't we let ideas stand or fall on their own merits? Jesus said, "You will know them by their fruits" (Matt 7:20).

In other words, judge things by the results they produce, not by their authority sources. People who are afraid to hear different doctrines or consider different ideas merely reveal their own lack of faith. Consider this parable: One man says, "I have the best racehorse in the world. In fact, it's the only perfect horse. All the other horses are wrong. However, I absolutely refuse to let him run in a free and open race. Instead, I insist upon locking the other entrants in their stalls or hobbling the few that do make it to the starting line. Mine and mine alone must be allowed upon the track!"

Another man says, "I, too, have a good racehorse. He performs well and compares favorably with others. I'll be delighted to let him run in a free and open race because I firmly believe if all of them are turned loose on the track, my horse will win!"

Now, which man has more faith in his horse?

In today's world, all views must be heard. All ideas must be considered. All doctrines must be analyzed. Otherwise, we'll never learn, grow, or make progress. If all the "horses" are allowed to run, we can be assured the "best one," which is truth, will win!

Two Liberals and a Conservative

Jesus once told a story about two liberals and a conservative. Now, of course, that's not what he called them. Those weren't the "code words" of his day; nevertheless, they exhibited all the classic traits.

Servant one had received five talents and gained five more. Servant two had received two talents and gained two more. The third servant had received one talent, which he buried.

Now, this third servant has often been criticized, but he would have had many supporters in that audience. In fact, according to Jewish Law, burying treasure was good! It absolved the person of all responsibility in case of loss. Burying was like putting things in a vault or a safety deposit box. Prudent people would say, "This guy did the right thing! After all, those other investors could have lost everything!" Corporations do go bankrupt! Banks do close their doors! Surely it was sensible to secure such a great trust. Surely protecting teachings and doctrines against heresy should be a high priority.

The religious leaders of that day saw themselves as preservers of the faith. They weren't interested in developing it or propagating it. Instead, it was their absolute duty to keep the Law and pass it on to the next generation. In a eulogy for a rabbi, the speaker told the grieving family, "Be of good comfort. He has given back intact the teachings which were entrusted to him." This was considered the highest good. This is exactly what the third servant did, saying, "You have what is yours" (Matt 25:25).

Surprisingly, however, Jesus said, "That's not good enough. You missed the whole point of life. You've failed in your spiritual obligation." In this parable Jesus is presenting a radically new teaching! For the first time, preserving and conserving are not rewarded! Jesus said, "The world doesn't need preservers. It needs riskers!" He said, "The kingdom doesn't need conservers of the status quo. It needs those who are brave enough to discover new truths, to try new methods, and to develop new possibilities. It needs people who are willing to put new wine in new wineskins and change the world!"

Useless Fruit Trees

It's a serious thing to live a useless life. Jesus had no patience with waste. He said, "A man had a fig tree planted in his vineyard, and he came looking for fruit on it and found none. So he said to the man working the vineyard, 'See here! For three years I have come looking for fruit on this fig tree, and still I find none. Cut it down! Why should it be wasting the soil?'" (Luke 13:6–7).

This deadbeat tree took up space that could have grown productive trees. It depleted the soil without contributing anything of value.

This tree that Jesus cursed had no figs, only leaves. That's a picture of a hypocrite. Each of us has one life to live—one brief opportunity to make a difference in this world. We can't afford to waste it. If Jesus cursed a useless fruit tree, how much more will he hold us accountable for a useless life?

Using Your Brain

During the Covid-19 pandemic, Christian congregations had to make difficult decisions about the best way to safely witness and worship. Some even viewed the situation as a "test of faith." They insisted upon meeting in large groups, breaking laws, and risking their health to demonstrate their dedication.

Fortunately, we don't have to choose between science and faith because Jesus faced a similar problem and set an example for us to follow. In the scriptures the tempter said, "If you are the Son of God, throw yourself down, for it is written, 'He will command his angels concerning you,' and 'On their hands they will bear you up, so that you will not dash your foot against a stone'" (Matt 4:5–6).

The tempter was saying, "If you are really God's Son, prove it! Test your faith, and the Lord will keep you from harm."

It's significant to discover that Jesus did not fall for this reckless suggestion. He knew God also gave us a brain, so he replied with another scripture, saying, "Again it is written, 'Do not put the Lord your God to the test'" (Matt 4:7; see also Deut 6:16).

His response shows us we are not supposed to do unreasonable things that break God's natural laws and then claim that we have God's protection. Instead, God expects us to have common Sense.

Furthermore, informed Christians know that we don't have to meet in large crowds to worship God. Jesus said, "Where two or three are gathered in my name, I am there among them" (Matt 18:20).

Walk as Jesus Walked

Many people only know that Jesus lay in a manger, walked on water, and hung on a cross. None of these facts help us very much because they can't be applied in our everyday lives. What we really need to know is how Jesus handled human emotions such as anger, greed, and fear. We need to know how Jesus made decisions. We need to know how he solved relationship problems. We need to know what purposes he wanted to accomplish. In short, we need to know how he faced difficult situations and lived a normal life.

It's unfortunate that most churches don't emphasize Jesus as a human being. They don't study his attitudes, words, actions, and lifestyle. But as followers we need to know what he thought, said, and did to discover how he wants us to live. The scripture says, "Whoever says, 'I abide in him,' ought to walk in the same way as he walked" (1 John 2:6).

Were Jesus's Prayers Always Answered?

Were Jesus's prayers always answered? This seems like a ridiculous and even irreverent question. At Lazarus's tomb, Martha certainly thought so. She said, "I know that God will give you whatever you ask of him" (John 11:22).

Nevertheless, it's obvious that some of his sincere requests were not granted. We know Jesus loved the rich young ruler and called him to be a disciple. Surely he prayed for him, yet the man walked away (see Mark 10:21–22). This man's free will took precedence over Jesus's sincere desire.

We also know the Lord was concerned about the people in Jerusalem. It's reasonable to assume he remembered them in prayer. Yet they would not respond (see Matt 23:37).

Fortunately, Jesus gave a statement that may explain this situation: "Father, I thank you for having heard me. I knew that you always hear me" (John 11:41–42).

Yes, God always hears, but he doesn't always provide the hoped-for answer. Humanity's free will can determine their choices and prevent some prayers from being answered. The consistency of universal principles and natural laws can also prevent some prayers from being answered.

When Jesus prayed those desperate prayers in Gethsemane, he begged, "My Father, if it is possible, let this cup pass from me" (Matt 26:39). But that didn't happen. Instead of removing the cup of suffering, Jesus was enabled to change his petition to say, "Your will be done!" (Matt 26:39).

A Woman's Place?

Many religions try to put women in their "place." Some Christians do this by quoting the Bible and laying guilt trips on liberated working women.

Do the scriptures really say, "A woman's place is in the home"? Hardly!

Miriam staged a public worship service: "The prophet Miriam, Aaron's sister, took a tambourine in her hand, and all the women went out after her with tambourines and with dancing" (Exod 15:20).

Deborah judged and led a nation in military conflicts: "Barak said to her, 'If you will go with me, I will go, but if you will not go with me, I will not go.' And she said, 'I will surely go with you; nevertheless, the road on which you are going will not lead to your glory, for the LORD will sell Sisera into the hand of a woman.' Then Deborah got up and went with Barak to Kedesh" (Judg 4:8–9).

Lydia was a successful merchant: "A certain woman named Lydia, a worshiper of God, was listening to us…. The Lord opened her heart to listen eagerly to what was said by Paul" (Acts 16:14).

Priscilla was a theologian and teacher: "Now there came to Ephesus a Jew named Apollos from Alexandria. He was an eloquent man, well-versed in the scriptures. He had been instructed in the Way of the Lord, and he spoke with burning enthusiasm and taught accurately the things concerning Jesus, though he knew only the baptism of John. He began to speak boldly in the synagogue, but when Priscilla and Aquila heard him they took him aside and explained the Way of God to him more accurately" (Acts 18:24–26).

Phoebe was a traveling church leader: "I commend to you our sister Phoebe, a deacon of the church at Cenchreae, so that you may welcome her in the Lord, as is fitting for the saints, and help her in whatever she may require from you" (Rom 16:1–2).

Jesus also gave a definitive statement about a woman's place, and it certainly wasn't "in the kitchen"! On the contrary, he indicated that Mary was doing a much better thing by thinking and talking than Martha was by cooking and cleaning.

So what do the scriptures teach about a woman's place? Well, that depends on which scripture you quote. Overall, however, the scriptures can't legitimately be used to restrict those females who wish to use their talents and abilities in areas other than homemaking.

A Woman's Role in Society

The role of women in society is an age-old biblical issue. One passage is clear about the role of women. In Proverbs 31 Solomon says

- A woman's place is in the factory: "She…works with willing hands" (v. 13).
- A woman's place is in shopping malls: "She seeks wool and flax…. She is like the ships of the merchant; she brings her food from far away" (vv. 13–14).
- A woman's place is in the real estate office: "She considers a field and buys it" (v. 16).
- A woman's place is in agriculture: "With the fruit of her hands she plants a vineyard" (v. 16).
- A woman's place is in charity bazaars: "She opens her hand to the poor and reaches out her hands to the needy" (v. 20).
- A woman's place is in crafts: "All her household are clothed in crimson. She makes herself coverings; her clothing is fine linen and purple" (vv. 21–22).
- A woman's place is in markets: "She makes linen garments and sells them; she supplies the merchant with sashes" (v. 24).
- This "ideal wife" is influential: "Her husband is known in the gates, when he sits among the elders of the land" (v. 23).
- This "ideal wife" is wise: "She opens her mouth with wisdom, and the teaching of kindness is on her tongue" (v. 26).
- This "ideal wife" is busy: "She looks well to the ways of her household and does not eat the bread of idleness" (v. 27).

In fact, this "model woman" is anything but a quiet, submissive housewife! Instead, she seems to be an ambitious, career-minded workaholic!

Words or Deeds?

Church worship today often consists of musical teams leading congregations in chanting phrases such as "We pour out our praise to Thee" and ending with raised hands and shouts of "Hallelujah!" Yet we have evidence that Jesus ridiculed and rejected such performances.

He said, "When you are praying, do not heap up empty phrases as the gentiles do, for they think that they will be heard because of their many words" (Matt 6:7).

He detested empty, pious words, saying, "Not everyone who says to me, 'Lord, Lord,' will enter the kingdom of heaven, but only the one who does the will of my Father in heaven" (Matt 7:21).

On another occasion he said, "This people honors me with their lips, but their hearts are far from me" (Matt 15:8).

Jesus was practical. He would agree with the old cowboy who expressed his opinion this way: "If I sat here on the porch all day and told everybody how wonderful my boss is and bragged about his ranch, I don't think he'd be pleased with me. No, siree! He'd rather I be out there feeding his cattle."

Worship must be more than words! One kind deed is worth more than a thousand hallelujahs.

Part 4:

Thinking About General Topics

Absolutism

As children we love our mothers, but when she frustrates us, we become angry. Since we haven't learned how to handle the concept that those who are good can sometimes also be bad, we tend toward absolutism. If this attitude continues, then as adults we'll see people as either totally good or totally bad. We'll see actions as either absolutely right or absolutely wrong.

Many people live in this rigid world. They alternate between excessive love and excessive hatred. They may idealize their friends and lovers, but when these individuals behave like normal, flawed human beings, they will completely reject them.

Such splitting is done by lovers who see women as either Madonnas or prostitutes. It's done by leaders who demand that followers must be either worshipers or enemies. Absolutism causes a person to be moody and inconsistent in their relationships.

A good/bad, right/wrong, on/off, yes/no universe is reassuring, but it's not realistic. We must recognize that it's possible for a person to be both worthy and unworthy at different times and at different places. It's possible to have feelings of hate intermingled with feelings of love. Absolutists ignore the gray areas. They polarize everything. They don't realize that most choices are between good and better or bad and worse.

Absolutism causes wild pendulum swings as a person moves from one extreme to the other. They are constantly hitting the walls because they don't know how to find a reasonable point somewhere in the middle.

As normal individuals mature, they learn how to live with ambivalence. Jesus said, "You are Peter, and on this rock I will build my church" (Matt 16:18), yet a short time later he said to Peter, "Get behind me, Satan! You are a stumbling hindrance to me" (Matt 16:23).

Ain't It Awful?

Today, many people are playing a sick psychological game called "Ain't It Awful?" Commentators, politicians, evangelists, and indeed entire populations fall into this trap.

Let's consider exactly what "good old days" we are sighing for. What other times were so much better? Do we want to return to our caveman ancestry, killing saber tooth tigers with rocks? Or join the Hebrew nomads wandering in the wilderness? Or would we like to live in that glorious century when gladiators fought to the death and Christians were torn by wild beasts to amuse Caesar?

Were those the "good old days"?

Oh, not those! Then perhaps we'd prefer the days when feudal lords and monarchs exercised the right of life or death, when starving children's hands were lopped off if they stole a loaf of bread, when eccentric grandmothers were burned as witches, when plagues wiped out whole civilizations, when one critical word resulted in torture!

If those weren't the "good old days" then, let's consider more recent times like the industrial revolution, when young people worked in coal mines; when slaves were sold like cattle; when civil war destroyed our land. Or maybe the Victorian era when women couldn't vote and modern appliances were unknown. Are we comparing our decade with the 1930s and the Dust Bowl depression? The 1940s with a world war and Nazism? The 1950s with Korea and McCarthyism? The 1960s with Vietnam, college riots, and burning cities?

Why are we so bent on this suicidal mentality? It's unfortunate that we don't trust our institutions and government, but is deadly cynicism the answer? The "ain't it awful" syndrome insinuates that somewhere else there is a utopia. Would we exchange places with people in Iran or Afghanistan? The poorest people in America live well by many cultural standards. Even slum dwellers today have luxuries that were unavailable to the rich of other centuries.

Of course we have problems! But it's ironic for Americans to sit in comfortable homes with full refrigerators and two cars, watching millionaires on TV play "Ain't It Awful?"

The power of negative thinking can lead to a self-fulfilling prophecy. If that happens, we may well experience a crisis so real that it would make us look back and long for these "good old days."

The psalmist had a different attitude. He expressed his appreciation by saying, "I will sing to the LORD because he has dealt bountifully with me" (Ps 13:6).

Believing It Doesn't Make It So

In their efforts to persuade, some people give the impression that if they can just get enough people to believe something, that will make it so! That's ridiculous! If fifty million people believe the earth is flat, it won't be any flatter than if no one believes it's flat! The earth is either flat or it's not flat. Our views on the subject are irrelevant. All reality is like that. Facts are stubborn things. They are unconcerned about the opinions of human beings. Truth is not determined by majority vote.

An old legend describes a cave that a busload of people decide to explore. Now, none of them know any details for sure. None have been there or know anyone who has been there. Nevertheless, fights about the truth of the matter cause delays in the fact-finding mission. Why are these travelers so illogical and defensive? Winning or losing the debates won't affect the end results. No amount of arguments will affect the end results. If all these people believe correctly about this matter, it isn't going to affect the end results. If all those people believe incorrectly, it still isn't going to affect the end results.

That cave is either there or it's not there. If all are right, they'll remain right. If only one is right, he'll remain right. So why can't each individual simply state an opinion, listen as others state their opinions, and then investigate the situation in a practical manner? If they do that, the truth as it really is—not as they think it is—will finally be known!

Solomon said, "Buy truth, and do not sell it" (Prov 23:23).

But Is It Right or Wrong?

Is it right to throw a baby out of a second-story window? You must answer "yes" or "no." Don't evade. Don't qualify. Surely if morals are absolute, you can respond to this simple question.

Well, not quite. Recently one man was given a medal for this very act while another man was sentenced to life imprisonment for the same act. How can that be? If situations make no difference, if circumstances never change the rightness or wrongness of a deed, then rewarding one and punishing another for the very same action was terribly unfair.

Of course, situations do make a difference, and circumstances do change the rightness or wrongness of a deed. The first man had rescued the child from a burning building. In this case, throwing the child out a window to firemen below was vastly better than leaving him to die in the flames. The other man had thrown a baby out of a window in a fit of rage at her mother.

Now, there was no difference in the acts. They were identical. The motives, however, were very different. One did the deed out of love, the other out of hate. The circumstances were also different. One did it as the lesser of two evils. When confronted with the choices of certain death in a burning building or the possibility of surviving even with injuries, the better decision is obvious.

Finally, the context was different and the question, taken out of that context, was misleading and impossible to answer. This proves that if you don't know the whole story, you can't respond with a simple "yes" or "no."

   Think (Or Else!)

When reporters force politicians to give thirty-second solutions to complex problems, they are encouraging shallow thinking. When people demand simplistic replies to profound questions, they are promoting misunderstanding.

Don't fall for these ploys. When adamant questioners insist on absolute answers, intelligent people will refuse to play the game.

Solomon said, "Get wisdom, and whatever else you get, get insight" (Prov 4:7).

The Danger of Conditioning

Biologists tell of an experiment with frogs. They say when they drop a frog into a pan of hot water, it immediately realizes the danger and hops out with little harm done. However, if they put a frog in a pan of tepid water and then gradually increase the temperature, the frog will sit there until it dies, never realizing that the water is getting too hot!

That's the power of conditioning! And that's a dangerous thing!

Paul described how the gradual wearing away of our internal alarm system, called the conscience, is an ever-present danger, saying, "Some will renounce the faith by paying attention to deceitful spirits…through the hypocrisy of liars whose consciences are seared with a hot iron" (1 Tim 4:1–2).

The Danger of Rigid Thought

People who are locked into a right/wrong, good/bad mentality are at risk because the world isn't like that. Life requires compromise and tolerance.

When incongruities are evident, when unfair situations exist, and when beliefs become incompatible with reality, a state of great dissonance develops. This makes individuals so miserable that adjustment is necessary. If such absolutists are unwilling to change their beliefs or adapt their outlook to fit reality, then compartmentalization occurs. When things don't fit together, they must be separated and put into watertight boxes. Religion becomes one box, work another box, family another, recreation another, and so on.

This is dangerous because it allows people to operate in certain areas without the benefit of their moral principles that are present in other areas. That's how criminals can be good church members, responsible fathers, helpful community leaders and still commit brutal murders. That's how terrorists can be virtuous within their religion and still commit atrocities on innocent people.

With complete compartmentalization, nothing seeps through the walls. Therefore, the logical thought processes, social guidelines, and compassionate feelings that may be present in one box can't influence the other boxes. These people no longer have wholeness or integrity since each area operates by its own set of rules and regulations.

This is a form of "split personality," but it's not defined as a psychotic illness because most of these individuals can still function. In fact, they may even be viewed as upright citizens and considered ideal examples of their special groups or cults. Also, they may be able to live a satisfactory life until a crisis occurs or the dissonance becomes unbearable.

Eventually, however, compartmentalization destroys us. Wholeness requires integration of all areas of life. It's the basis for health and happiness and productivity. When our beliefs are at odds with truth or reality, it's our beliefs that must change. Fanatical, rigid people can't change, and that leads to tragedy.

Solomon said, "Those who ignore instruction despise themselves, but those who heed admonition gain understanding" (Prov 15:32).

The Deadly Seesaw

Some people say, "If this is wrong, then its opposite must be right!" That's a common assumption, and yet it's a great fallacy! In fact, if this is wrong, then its opposite is probably equally wrong! If three hundred degrees above zero is destructive to the human body, then would its opposite, three hundred degrees below zero, be exactly the right temperature? Of course not! Extremes are usually equally destructive.

Solomon said, "Give me neither poverty nor riches" (Prov 30:8). He explained that being poor might cause him to steal and being wealthy might make him deny God.

This either/or mentality is applied in many areas. It happens in the battle between superstitions and science, the spirit and the mind, and the religious realm and the secular realm. Because so many traditional doctrines elevate blind faith over facts and orthodox rules over reality, the intellectual community has often repudiated or ignored all Christianity.

Unfortunately, this may be just as irrational as following a gullible ideology. It can cause mistakes just as deadly as the one it is trying to avoid.

It's true, superstition must be abolished, but it's also true that many Christian doctrines can be reinterpreted in such a way that their valid concepts are retained. This inclusive approach allows people to draw on the strength of their spiritual heritage.

Many people still need the stability and comfort of their religious ties, but those ties don't have to include invalid notions. The assumption that people have to abandon their faith to retain their credibility in a secular world is false.

Unfortunately, choosing an either/or position is easier than developing a both/and lifestyle! The current "two ends of the seesaw" mentality is producing polarization and conflict. If each group keeps trying to exterminate the other, then nothing will be accomplished.

Deprivation or Gratification?

The attitudes and habits of older Americans were formed by both the Great Depression and the rural, non-technological world. Daily tasks included chopping wood, hanging out clothes, canning vegetables, and sewing homemade dresses and shirts. Water was heated on wood stoves, and cows were milked by hand. There were no air conditioners, no indoor bathrooms, and no electric lights.

Debt was suspect, and welfare and credit cards were unknown. Paying cash caused these men and women to make a direct connection between earning and spending. After World War II the economy improved, but that generation still remembered the hard times and feared their return.

Most younger Americans, on the other hand, have never seen hard times. Instead, personal satisfaction is their theme. That's why statements such as these sound reasonable: "I want it; therefore, I'll buy now and pay later"; "If my job is disagreeable, I'll quit it and find another one"; "I'm tired of work, so I'll take off a year and 'find myself.'"

Since outlooks are shaped by experience, our society today reflects two extremes: the fears of deprivation and the demands for gratification. This explains the enormous generation gap. When our senior citizens are gone, we will lose an important reminder of the value of work and the rewards of economic responsibility!

Job asked, "Is wisdom with the aged and understanding in length of days?" (Job 12:12). We can answer: "Yes!"

Discretion

There's an old story about a man who had three sons. The father wanted to teach the boys a lesson in discretion, so he gave each of them a partially rotten apple. The first ate his apple, rotten spots and all. The second saw the rotten spots and threw the entire apple away. The third carefully cut out the rotten parts and ate the good parts.

That's discernment. Few things are perfect in this imperfect world. Therefore, we must not expect every opinion or every situation or every opportunity or even every person to be perfect in every way. Neither should we reject good ideas or opportunities or people just because they have some imperfections. What we need most is a rational spirit of discretion in evaluating, choosing, and salvaging that which is good.

Solomon prayed, "Give your servant, therefore, an understanding mind to govern your people, able to discern between good and evil" (1 Kgs 3:9).

Don't Be Fooled

It's easy to arouse the public with fear tactics. It's easy to rally support with emotional calls for a return to the "good old days." It's easy to influence the masses by claiming that excited crowds and loud noises are synonymous with truth and success. But using such simplistic criteria has several serious flaws. It certainly has no historical basis. Over the years, those who were right were seldom popular, and those who were popular were seldom right.

Noah gained no followers. Elijah was a minority facing four hundred fifty false prophets (see 1 Kgs 18:22). Jeremiah was one lone voice in a dungeon. None of these show up well when measured by current criteria of success.

Hitler, on the other hand, had a tremendous following. Stalin drew throngs of dedicated devotees. Putin has a ninety percent approval rating. Popularity is never proof of validity. Jesus said true prophets are not necessarily popular (see Mark 6:4). In fact, his own followers left him in droves (see John 6:66).

Jesus was rejected. The scripture says, "His own people did not accept him" (see John 1:11).

In fact, the scripture says, "All of them deserted [Jesus] and fled" (see Mark 14:50).

So was Jesus a failure? Was Jesus a loser? Of course not, because popularity and temporary success are never proofs of validity. That's why modern-day politicians who tell the truth often get defeated while those who say what the people want to hear often get elected.

Research shows that only about one third of all people really think. The emotional fervor of a crowd in no way proves the truth of the speaker's message.

Jesus said, "Woe to you when all speak well of you" (Luke 6:26).

Be a thinker! Don't be fooled by hype!

Don't Be Gullible

It's amazing that an itinerant preacher with limited funds would discourage a wealthy person from making a contribution to his ministry. Yet Jesus did just that when he counseled the rich young ruler to "sell your possessions, and give the money to the poor…. Then come, follow me" (Matt 19:21).

Can you imagine one of today's TV evangelists or megachurch pastors giving such advice? Couldn't Jesus and his disciples have used this man's wealth to spread the gospel? Of course they could! Why, then, did he tell the man to give everything away before joining his group?

In fact, Jesus despised the trappings of power and possessions. He commended the poor widow's mite and denigrated the rich man's fortune. He constantly sought to separate worship from wealth.

It's significant that the only incident of physical violence in Jesus's life was aimed at the religious leaders who made money at the expense of the people. He knew that when greed enters the picture, houses of prayer become dens of thieves!

It's strange that some modern preachers who claim to follow Jesus so fanatically in other matters totally depart from him when it comes to finances. Indeed, on the subject of money, they often take the opposite position, saying, "Support me and my crusade."

It's also significant that Jesus never promised material rewards to those who followed him. He never gave hopes of fabulous windfalls. He did not promote a prosperity gospel. He never insinuated that the faithful would find unexpected checks in their mailboxes. Instead, he was an honest realist. He said, "You'll probably be persecuted! You may lose your family, your land, your houses, or even your life, but following truth and promoting justice is its own reward."

Perhaps we should use Jesus's criteria in evaluating religious leaders and institutions. Perhaps we should ask, "Is this organization interested in me or my money?" Remember, Jesus said, "Dispose of all your possessions, and then come follow me!" Therefore, if someone expresses the opposite advice, saying, "Come follow me, and then I'll help you dispose of your possessions," beware! Jesus warned us over and over again not to be gullible!

Don't Decide Too Soon

Often, when we hear one person's view of an issue, it sounds so reasonable and persuasive that we agree and take a stand! Once we've done this, it becomes almost impossible to change. We now have a position to defend and an ego to protect. Therefore, when we hear a different view of the issue, we're prejudiced against it and almost obligated to oppose it.

Such premature decisions are unfortunate. Many problems occur because people take sides and stake out positions before they know all the facts. It's much better to hear and analyze, or to hear and consider, than it is to hear and decide. We don't have to immediately agree or disagree with anything. Instead, we can hang loose. We can reserve judgment. We can wait and see.

We need to realize that it's possible to love and support people without espousing all their beliefs and authenticating all their grievances. In fact, if we're tactful, we may even be able to broaden their views and soften their complaints. We can point out other possibilities. We can provide more information. We can show different perspectives.

Intelligent people are slow to take irrevocable stands. They know it's easier to be objective before you have a position to defend and an ego to protect. So don't decide too soon!

Solomon encourages us to listen and understand: "If one gives answer before hearing, it is folly and shame" (Prov 18:13).

Don't Go to Extremes

Nature likes the middle ground. Drastic aberrations from the norm are not usually passed on in the genetic code. Extremes are perceived as dangerous. Therefore, one of the absolute principles of life is that if people or systems don't control themselves, someone or something else will do it for them.

The flip side of rights is responsibilities, and these must balance to be productive. If social media, movies, and TV keep pushing their "freedom" to atrocious and outrageous limits, they'll eventually be censored. If individuals or protest groups keep pushing their "freedom" by including terrorism and arson and murder, they'll go to jail. If workers keep pushing toward higher and higher wages, they'll eventually bankrupt the company.

Pushing the limits is a natural human response, but it's not mature or productive. We need to set our own limits and exercise our own discipline. If we don't do it ourselves, then others will do it for us. Paul gives advice about that, saying, "Exercise self-control in all things" (1 Cor 9:25).

Drawing Lines

Almost every issue gets reduced to one question: "Is it right or wrong?" So easy! And yet so impossible to answer. Furthermore, as soon as you express a tolerant attitude, you're instantly confronted with this rebuttal: "But where do you draw the line?" How simplistic. As if life were laid out in neat, precise lines.

We seem to be preoccupied with setting boundaries. All of this would be much less hazardous if you really could draw a line and leave it there forever. But life changes, circumstances shift, and situations differ.

Invariably, those carefully constructed lines have to be redrawn. This creates a problem, because once you've established your territory and drawn your lines, it's natural for you to want them to stay there. But they don't.

Life is real. It isn't dependable and static. The need for absolutes will never be met. The insistence upon neat, immovable lines will never be realized. People who cling to these unrealistic expectations become miserable, judgmental misfits.

So where do you draw the line? Wherever the greatest good can be realized at the moment. But be ready to redraw those lines if you become wiser or circumstances change.

When they hear this advice, some people object, saying, "That's hedonism." That's an "anything goes" philosophy. That's "doing what you feel like" morality. Even so, you must constantly redraw the lines.

In fact, you do constantly redraw the lines. For instance, when you need to drive a nail and all you have available is a brick, you use it. It becomes the right tool for the moment. However, if you later find a hammer, you'd be a fool to refuse to use it just because the brick had once been the right tool. That's true of many things, and it's not immoral to change the rules and redraw the lines as circumstances change!

Paul adapted to different cultures and circumstances. He said, "I have become all things to all people, that I might by all means save some" (1 Cor 9:22).

Examine the Fruit

Scams and frauds are common today. Fortunately, Jesus gave us an ironclad rule to test such situations. He said, "Beware of false prophets, who come to you in sheep's clothing but inwardly are ravenous wolves. You will know them by their fruits.... Every good tree bears good fruit, but the bad tree bears bad fruit. A good tree cannot bear bad fruit, nor can a bad tree bear good fruit" (Matt 7:15–18).

This valuable and practical advice tells us how to make wise, moral decisions. It helps us decide who to trust and who to distrust. It says, "Don't succumb to exciting propaganda." It says, "Don't just admire an attractive tree with lots of colorful leaves. Instead, evaluate its fruit!"

A person's words may sound great, and their promises may be rosy, but if the details are vague, then it is probably suspect. Talk is cheap! Actions matter! Leaders who try to influence people with emotional appeals are false and dangerous. They know how to overrule your reason and logic. They know that if they can instill feelings of fear and anger, it will shut down your cognitive system and cause you to revert to animalistic survival instincts.

When you are confronted with such tactics, always ask yourself these questions: If this situation continues and escalates, will it encourage peace or chaos? Will it increase love or hatred? Will it lead to sensible permanent solutions or to irrational temporary reactions?

If the fruit of this tree is not productive and positive, then no matter how satisfying it appears for the moment, its fruit is bad and must be avoided. Jesus believed trees with inedible fruit should be chopped down. He said, "Every tree that does not bear good fruit will be cut down and thrown into the fire. Thus you will know them by their fruits" (Matt 7:19–20).

Goals and Detours

A straight line may be the shortest distance between two points, but that route may not be the best choice. A superhighway may cut down on the driving time between two cities, but that highway may miss some important sights along the way. Sometimes great treasures are off the beaten path. Sometimes the goals you're trying to reach are only to be found through detours.

Paul and Silas were headed to Bithynia, but they ended up in Macedonia (see Acts 16:7–9). As a result of this "detour," Lydia and her household and the jailer and his household were reached with the gospel.

Predetermined, "efficient" routes aren't always the most productive or the most enjoyable. If you go straight from New York to Los Angeles, you'll miss the Grand Canyon. If you go straight from Philadelphia to Detroit, you'll miss Niagara Falls. If you go straight from Dallas to Winnipeg, you'll miss Mt. Rushmore.

So when your plans are upset, when your schedules are changed, when you must take a detour, don't despair. Look upon it as an adventure, not an adversity. Look upon it as an opportunity, not an obstacle. Look upon it as a possibility, not a problem.

If you stay alert and positive, you may reach some unexpected goals because of your detours.

   Think (Or Else!)

Homeostasis

All living things seek homeostasis, a balanced state in which an organism needs nothing. Trying to reach such an ideal situation motivates everything we do. When we're cold, we shiver to raise our temperature. When we're hot, we sweat to lower our temperature. This same balance is needed in all areas of life, but it's hard to find and even harder to maintain.

As human beings we are erratic. We can't seem to discover a middle ground. We bounce from one extreme to another. We don't know how to set our own limits, so we push until some disaster stops us. Wild pendulum swings determine our course. Moderation is an elusive goal. So we get on a roller coaster ride of ups and downs.

Also, we don't understand that life is a package deal. There's always a liability for every asset and a negative for every positive. You have to buy both sides of an old record album to get one special song. Sometimes life is like that.

This is an imperfect world, and compromises are necessary. Finding that middle ground requires reason and common sense.

The scriptures stress the fact that being satisfied is a desirable trait. Paul said, "I have learned to be content with whatever I have" (Phil 4:11).

How Manipulators Handle Criticism

In our world today, manipulators are common and dangerous. They operate as controllers and propagandists. When people confront or criticize them for their destructive acts, they become defensive and even violent.

First, they deny it by claiming that it didn't even happen. They look shocked and totally innocent. They claim that their critic is evil and only out to destroy them.

Second, they distort it by muddying the water, twisting the words, spinning the information, and increasing confusion,

Next, they divert it by pointing to others' mistakes and saying, "That's worse."

Then, they doubt it by minimizing its importance and ignoring its negative consequences. They may even release a few obvious incriminating details quickly before their opponent can accuse them. But they refuse to admit guilt or apologize,

Finally, they disclose it by normalizing the behavior, saying, "Of course we did that, but so what? We had every right to do it. It's been done before. Everyone else does it. Why are we even discussing this?"

If all else fails, they may use the old political trick of "creating a crisis." They stir up emotion and make a lot of noise about it. Then they do something to alleviate the problem or simply declare it solved and claim total credit for achieving a great victory.

Therefore, try to avoid people who use these tactics. Jesus knew we would encounter such dangerous individuals. He said, "I am sending you out like sheep into the midst of wolves, so be wise as serpents" (Matt 10:16).

I'm a Liberal, Moderate, Conservative Fundamentalist

Words and labels are used so glibly! Nevertheless, labels will obviously include different concepts for different people. So with this in mind, I will declare myself a liberal, moderate, conservative fundamentalist.

I'm liberal because I'm open to new truth and tolerant of diversity.

I'm moderate because I believe extremes are usually destructive and compromise is essential.

I'm conservative because I hold on tenaciously to those things that have proven to be valid and productive in my life

I'm a fundamentalist because I rest my ideology on a few definite, crucial concepts.

These are my fundamentals:

- I believe this is a unified universe. There are no separate islands of knowledge or ultimate conflicts. All are connected.
- I believe there are consistent principles. There are no illogical, arbitrary events. Causes and consequences are inexorably linked.
- I believe in a moral God. There are no chosen people, elect groups, or unfair responses.
- I believe in individualized salvation. No one formula can effect change in everyone. Each person must realize his own worth in his own way.
- I believe there is a relative ethical system. Absolute standards do exist, but since earthly situations vary, tradeoffs and mixed motives are inevitable.

Philosophically, I'm liberal. Socially, I'm moderate. Economically, I'm conservative. Theologically, I'm a fundamentalist. Yet I dare anybody to categorize me into one of these popular boxes. I dare anybody to stereotype me with one of these popular labels. In fact, all people are like that. Human beings are bigger and more complex than labels.

Paul said, "Let no evil talk come out of your mouths but only what is good for building up" (Eph 4:29).

Instinct or Reason?

Human beings are motivated by both instinct and reason. Unfortunately, reason is often less influential because it's a fairly recent development. Instinct, on the other hand, originated at the beginning of life. It's concerned with the survival and propagation of the species, not necessarily with the welfare of each individual. This can cause problems in a technological world.

For example, in primitive times, a quick, reflexive physical reaction saved people from tigers and snakes and bears. You had to get him before he got you! Today, it's no longer a survival mechanism. Instead, a quick, reflexive physical reaction causes gun violence, road rage, and domestic abuse.

In primitive times, suppression of deviants was also important because one odd member threatened the whole group. A white deer in a brown herd attracted predators. A crippled person kept the tribe from moving efficiently. Misfits hindered progress. Today, suppression of deviancy is no longer a survival mechanism. Instead, it causes prejudice, intolerance, and bigotry.

In primitive times, suspicion of strangers was understandable. Those who didn't look like "us" and dress like "us" and believe like "us" must be an enemy. Conformity, unity, and solidarity offered protection to those vulnerable groups. Today, an "us vs. them" mentality is no longer a survival mechanism. Instead, it causes racial riots, religious persecution, and civil wars.

Many other "instincts" that were once "species positive" are now "humanity negative." Promiscuous males ensured the proliferation of their genetic code. Now this behavior leads to disease, broken families, and overpopulation.

A subservient, submissive "slave mentality" kept people from being annihilated by all powerful rulers. Now this attitude keeps citizens from exercising the autonomy needed in a democracy.

Using resources immediately was important because they would either deteriorate or be stolen. Now this habit encourages impulsivity, debt, and an absence of deferred gratification habits.

Being motivated by vestiges of primitive instincts can be deadly. We must learn to let reason override these unproductive urges.

God invites us to use logical thought, saying, "Come now, let us argue it out" (Isa 1:18).

Knowing When to Stop

"Give her an inch, and she'll take a mile!"; "He always goes overboard!"; "They never know when to stop!"

Some of these old adages are valid. Many of life's evils are caused by pushing things too far. Any virtue can become a vice if it's carried to extremes. For example, employers were once "masters," and employees were "slaves." Working conditions were awful, wages were low, and safety was ignored. Then the employees began to organize unions and demand rights. Their working conditions improved, safety regulations were enacted, and wages rose.

Unfortunately, some didn't know when to stop! That's human nature. Whatever you make, it's never enough! If pushed too far, companies either go bankrupt or move to foreign countries with cheaper labor. So the employees who had once received too little and then received too much may be unemployed, now receiving nothing.

Everything seems to be like that! Over and over, we see individuals, groups, and nations that suffer from oppression and discrimination. They protest and make some progress, but then they go too far until they become the oppressors.

In politics and religious idealism, we push conservatism, but it's never conservative enough for fanatics. So we continue until life forces our hand and we go liberal, and it's never liberal enough for the radicals. So we continue seesawing until we create chaos!

Why can't we learn when to stop? Why must we always push until we crash and thus set up a destructive overreaction?

Bureaucracies always get more complex. Offices always get more technological. Executives always get bigger expense accounts. Things always grow until a revolt or a catastrophe brings things to a screeching halt. Why must we always let crises set our agenda? Why must we always go to extremes?

Knowing when to stop is the basis of all wisdom. It's obvious that moderation is a value. If taking two aspirins is good, then is taking one hundred better? Of course not! It's deadly. If lowering the room temperature in summer ten degrees is good, then is lowering it a hundred degrees better? Of course not! Why can't we use common sense in all areas of life and stop before we overdo things?

Just once, why doesn't someone say, "No! My salary is fair, so instead of a raise, let's put the money elsewhere and improve the business." Just once, why doesn't someone say, "No! This insurance settlement is adequate. Let's not sue for an exorbitant amount and ultimately raise all rates." Just once, why doesn't someone say, "No! I don't need more assistants and computers to do my job well. So let's not wreck our economy by asking for enormous budget increments!"

Pipe dreams? Maybe! But it's a necessity if we're to survive as a society. Somebody must know when to stop! That's difficult, because with material things there's never enough. The scriptures say, "The lover of money will not be satisfied with money, nor the lover of wealth with gain" (Eccl 5:10).

Me and My Rights

Many people's definition of the first amendment is "legislation that allows anyone to say anything I think is right."

Many people's definition of academic freedom is "the license to teach any philosophy I agree with."

Many people's definition of democracy is "a place where all individuals who look and act like me are extended justice and equality."

In fact, these definitions describe a dictator state. People in Iran can say anything the ruler thinks is right. People in Russia can teach any philosophical view that the Kremlin agrees with. People in Nazi Germany extended justice to all those individuals who looked and acted like Hitler.

The first amendment, the principle of academic freedom, and a democratic system are entirely different. They guarantee that people are even allowed to say things I think are wrong! They guarantee that teachers and writers and speakers have the freedom to express views the power structures don't agree with. Above all, they guarantee that justice and equality must be extended even to those "misguided misfits" who don't look or act at all like me and other members of my social group.

Such is the unique and wonderful and often misunderstood definition of America. Citizens of a democracy should follow Paul's advice: "Do not seek your own advantage but that of the other" (1 Cor 10:24).

The Moderate Middle

Strangely enough, extreme liberals and extreme conservatives are not opposites. Instead, they're twins under the skin. In fact, they are indistinguishable when it comes to three basic principles.

All extremists oversimplify issues and demand absolute answers. Things must be black or white. There are no grays. Things are either perfectly good or completely evil.

All extremists condemn and indeed try to exterminate those who have different beliefs and agendas. They can't disagree without being disagreeable.

All extremists consider individuals to be expendable; therefore, they subordinate them to their ideology.

Jesus, on the other hand, was in the "moderate middle." His mission was equally at odds with the Sadducees, who represented one extreme, and the Pharisees, who represented another extreme.

Jesus never practiced absolutism. He was flexible when it came to traditions and taboos.

Jesus was not prejudiced. He associated with people who represented a wide range of races, religions, and lifestyles. He saw good in Samaritans. He saw wisdom in Syro-Phoenicians. He saw faith in Roman centurions.

Jesus never subordinated the needs of individual people to rules and creeds. He forgave the woman taken in adultery. He ate with publicans and sinners. He allowed his followers to pick and eat grain on the Sabbath and omitted fasting when it wasn't practical.

Let's avoid either/or extremes. Very cold temperatures can kill you, but so can very hot temperatures. In America, groups are becoming polarized politically, religiously, and economically. That's not productive in a democracy. To accomplish anything we must work together in the "moderate middle."

The scripture reminds us that we are working together with God (see 2 Cor 6:1).

Nothing Is All Bad

Nothing is all bad. Every dark cloud has a silver lining, and it's our job to find its bright side. Joseph understood this principle when he said to his brothers, who had sold him into slavery, "Do not be distressed or angry with yourselves because you sold me here…. Even though you intended to do harm to me, God intended it for good" (Gen 45:5; 50:20).

A philosopher said, "Every problem contains the seeds of its own solution." Most of us feel that life would be simply wonderful if we had easier problems or fewer problems or, better still, no problems at all. But that's not necessarily true. Always remember that to every disadvantage there is a corresponding advantage.

There's an old story about two shoe salesmen who traveled to a primitive country. When they got off the ship, hundreds of barefoot natives greeted them. Both salesmen rushed to send a telegram. The first one wired his company, "Am returning home immediately. Nobody wears shoes here." The second salesman sent an equally urgent message to his company. It read, "Send me all the merchandise you have! Nobody has shoes here."

These two men faced the same situation, but they had opposite points of view. One saw the challenge as a negative and retreated. The other saw the challenge as a positive and advanced.

Nothing is all bad!

Of Mudslinging and Politics

Granny said, "If you can't say something good about somebody, don't say anything at all."

Solomon said, "Whoever utters slander is a fool" (Prov 10:18).

Paul said, "Speak evil of no one" (Titus 3:2).

James said, "Do not speak evil against one another" (Jas 4:11).

Jesus warned, "On the day of judgment you will have to give an account for every careless word you utter" (Matt 12:36).

Are we obeying these injunctions? It certainly doesn't seem so. Maybe that's what's wrong with America. Every year, or two years, or four years, or six years, politicians come out slinging mud, belittling, maligning, slandering, and accusing. For months on end, we hear nothing but criticism and name-calling. Characters are assassinated, records are perverted, and nothing positive is mentioned. We hear liberals vilifying conservatives and conservatives vilifying liberals. Through media saturation these doomsday messages are repeated over and over again. No wonder, as citizens, we become angry and demoralized.

What do you suppose would happen to America if we all followed this scriptural admonition? "Whatever is true, whatever is honorable, whatever is just, whatever is pure, whatever is pleasing, whatever is commendable, if there is any excellence and if there is anything worthy of praise, think about these things" (Phil 4:8).

Of Rewards and Results

We get what we reward. Over and over, researchers have demonstrated that the behavior of living things can be shaped by using a system of incentives and disincentives.

A pigeon was put in a cage equipped so he would receive a grain of corn if he pecked on a certain spot. At first the pigeon pecked all over the floor at random. Eventually, he accidentally tripped the release mechanism. He didn't know exactly what he had done to produce the food, but he gradually began to peck in the general area of the trigger. Every time he hit the spot successfully and was rewarded with corn, he became a little more efficient and specific. Finally, he ignored all the other areas and went straight to the spot that released his corn.

Human beings are like that. Cultures are like that. Civilizations are like that. This pigeon illustrates a universal principle. The principle is that we tend to repeat actions that reward us and neglect actions that don't reward us. This principle explains why certain nations, cultures, and individuals develop some traits and lose others.

In short, what each group needed and valued and rewarded has developed, and what they didn't need or value or reward has been neglected. This principle explains why America has more football players than philosophers. It explains why we have better technicians than theologians. It explains why there are more soap operas than classics and more sensational tabloids than logical journals. It explains why magazines report gossip instead of information and our political reporters emphasize sex scandals instead of in-depth analysis.

This principle also explains why some religions attract nonproductive people. That's why institutions that value and reward obedience and submission will never develop autonomous, original thinkers.

If we understand these developmental processes, we can plan our future. We can decide what values we want and what skills we need and begin to reward those who exemplify these traits. If we do this, the desired values and skills will develop. This principle is dependable. This principle works! We get what we reward!

Paul said, "Each will receive wages according to their own labor" (1 Cor 3:8).

Ox Carts and Wagons

Wagons are better than ox carts, but they are not as efficient as automobiles. When we study history, we don't ridicule either ox carts or wagons because we know each of them provided the best transportation available at the time.

Ox carts weren't wrong in 3000 BC. They were right! Wagons weren't wrong in AD 1800. They were right! But they are not the best modes of transportation now.

Likewise, Moses's laws about punishment (see Lev 24:16; Deut 13:6–10; 21:18–21; 22:20–21) weren't necessarily wrong in the Old Testament era. They were probably as right as their social development would allow at the time. Paul's admonitions about slavery (see Eph 6:5; Col 3:22) weren't necessarily wrong in AD 70. They were probably as right as their cultural situation would allow at the time. But these laws and admonitions are not right for our day when we have more maturity and better information.

This progressive revelation explains how, even though these "inspired scriptures" were as valid as they could be at the time they were written, that doesn't mean we are still obligated to follow them today.

Inspiration doesn't mean the insights of the ancients are valid for all time. We applaud them for each progressive thought but realize that if some of these thoughts were put into practice today, they would be regressive. We need to be conservative of every valid precept, but we also need to be liberal when decisions can be based on new knowledge and new circumstances.

So even as wagons replaced ox carts and cars replaced wagons, better methods of transportation will probably replace cars someday. Each is right for its time, but none is right for all time. Likewise, some doctrines and practices, even though they may have served the religious community well in the past, need to be replaced.

Reality or Perception?

Do we believe in reality, or do we believe in our perception of reality? Do we believe in things as they are, or do we believe in things as we've been told they are? Do we believe in facts, or do we believe in stereotypes?

These are significant questions, because clever manipulation can "create" perceptions. If a candidate can associate his opponent with negative words and images, he can paint a character picture that doesn't exist.

If an advertiser can repeat a brand name often enough or get a famous person to endorse it, he can make a bestseller out of a lemon. If a speaker is skillful in the use of emotional stories and code phrases, he can persuade his listeners to abandon their common sense.

In fact, Americans base their attitudes and actions on perception to a frightening degree! Most of us don't know what we think until the polls or the authority figures tell us!

That's why Jesus warned us to be as wise as serpents (see Matt 10:16).

Saints or Scoundrels?

Goethe once said, "It's a pity the Lord made only one man of me. There's material aplenty for both a saint and a scoundrel!" Indeed, that's true of everyone. We're all moral mixtures.

> There's so much good in the worst of us
> And so much bad in the best of us
> That it ill behooves a few of us
> To criticize the rest of us!

Individuals, organizations, religions, nations, and life itself contain these paradoxical elements. That's why propaganda is possible. That's why advertisement is successful. That's why gossip is believable. We can zero in on the constructive aspects or the destructive aspects of anyone or anything. It's easy to emphasize some points and omit other points. By picking and choosing and arranging information we can create a picture that is *factually* true but *actually* false. Such slanting is deceptive. It takes the whole truth to be truth.

That's why Solomon said, "Buy truth, and do not sell it" (Prov 23:23).

That's why Jesus said, "I am the way and the truth and the life" (John 14:6).

That's why Paul said, "Whatever is true…think about these things" (Phil 4:8).

Seeing from a Different Perspective

Once, a pecan harvester learned an important principle. He picked up every nut he could see. As he stood and surveyed the leaf-covered ground, he saw absolutely none! Strangely enough, however, he found that if he moved around to another side and looked, he could see many, many more nuts that had not been visible from the first perspective.

Likewise, you can't see all of life from one perspective. You must move around to get other viewpoints. The best way to do that is by listening and learning from different philosophies and cultures. The scripture says, "My people are destroyed for lack of knowledge!" (Hos 4:6).

Sex and Violence

We watch television, listen to the radio, read newspapers, use the internet and ask, "Why is there so much sex and violence?" Well, there is a reason, and that reason is within each of us!

You see, everyone has a deep need for love, and instead of getting that need filled with the healthy nurture of parents and spouses and friends, we seek to fill it vicariously. This leads to perversions and obsessions. But soap operas, romance novels, and pornography are poor substitutes for the real love we're starved for.

Everyone wants power, but instead of attaining positions of legitimate control, we identify with superheroes and winners.

Everyone wants excitement, but instead of researching and developing challenging scientific and theological insights, we satisfy our curiosity with UFOs and demons.

Then everyone has a large reservoir of unresolved anger. Instead of dealing with our hostilities in an open and productive way, we express our desire for revenge vicariously through watching and identifying with clever criminals and alien warriors.

Our media and entertainment will become more positive and productive if we as individuals learn to fill our human needs in positive and productive ways, instead of denying those needs and seeking cheap substitutes in the media.

Paul said, "Have nothing to do with profane and foolish tales" (1 Tim 4:7).

Symbols

The flag isn't America! You don't destroy America by destroying a flag. You don't strengthen America by saluting the flag. Freedom is more than a physical object.

We must not confuse truth with the emblems we've designed to represent truth. The flag only represents democracy to those who consider it so.

Likewise, loving America so much that we punish those who don't undermines the spirit of democracy.

Dedication to America and its flag must be voluntary. Otherwise, it's a dictatorship in disguise. True freedom includes the right to disagree. Unless democracy is strong enough to withstand opposition, it's worthless.

Those who burn the flag don't do nearly as much damage to the cause of freedom as those who would punish those who burn the flag. If we were as eager to fight for the principles of freedom as we are to fight for the symbols of freedom, we'd be better off.

Symbols are exactly that—symbols. They must not be treated as idols. The meaning of a symbol lies in the eye of the beholder. For instance, to some Southerners the Confederate flag represents their heritage and history. To African Americans it's racist. To foreigners it's just a piece of cloth.

The cross is important to Christians. The star of David is important to Jews. Medals and badges and trophies each have specific emotions associated with them. Nevertheless, those things are still merely symbols.

Loving God so much that you punish those who don't undermines the spirit of Christianity.

Wearing a cross doesn't make you a Christian. Carrying a Bible doesn't make you a moral person.

Let's use common sense and never forget that symbols are created by human beings. They are given their significance by human beings. They should not become articles of worship!

Jesus gave no credence to sacred items. He ridiculed those who wore boxes of scriptures on their forehead and long fringes on their prayer garments (see Matt 23:5).

He gave no credence to sacred places, saying, "You will worship the Father neither on this mountain nor in Jerusalem" (John 4:21).

He gave no credence to sacred words, saying, "Not everyone who says to me, 'Lord, Lord,' will enter the kingdom of heaven" (Matt 7:21).

Instead, Jesus urged us to worship a God of "spirit and truth" (see John 4:24).

Three-Dimensional Thinking

The question isn't, "To think or not to think?" Everybody thinks! Instead, the question is, "How do we think?"

First, we must think broader. Don't base your conclusions on one side or two sides of an issue. There is an infinite number of "sides." Things are so complex that we need to get various perspectives before attempting to define reality. Avoid flat, either/or thinking. Opposites are not the only options. Two extremes don't average out to perfection. A man with one foot on a hot stove and one foot on a piece of ice is not comfortable. The opposite of obesity is starvation, and neither one is desirable. Avoid a seesaw mentality. It's fallacious! You don't have to put man down to put God up.

Second, we must think deeper. Don't base your conclusions on superficial observations. There is always more than meets the eye. See beneath the surface. Examine, analyze, and make connections. There are no "islands" of knowledge. This perception is misleading. When you fly over Hawaii, the islands below look like separate entities, but if you were able to go deep enough, you'd find they are all connected to one planet. Likewise, when you survey various subjects such as biology, theology, physics, and geology, they look like separate entities, but if you dig down, you'll find that these things are parts of the whole.

Third, we must think longer. Don't base your conclusions on immediate data alone. Realize that seeds become trees, and babies become men, and little mistakes become fatal catastrophes. You shouldn't build a doghouse to fit the puppy! He will grow! Take the long view. Set up a hypothetical chain of events. Project causes to their logical consequences. Note actions and the probable effects of those actions. Consider all future implications. Ask, "Is this course likely to lead to dead-end streets or open roads?"

Three-dimensional thinking will lead to valid, productive decisions! Jesus asked a three-dimensional question, saying, "What do you think of the Messiah?" (Matt 22:42).

As usual, such a profound question stymied these critics, and the scripture says, "No one was able to give him an answer, nor from that day did anyone dare to ask him any more questions" (Matt 22:46).

    Think (Or Else!)

Trusting Your Feelings

Some feelings are instincts and urges. These are hard-wired into us—fear and anger ensure our self-preservation. Other feelings come from experience and events in our lives. If something threatens us, we will be afraid of that in the future.

But feelings can be confusing. Someone said, "If a cat sits on a hot stove, it will avoid hot stoves in the future. Unfortunately, however, it will probably avoid cold stoves too." That's how phobias develop. If pain occurs at a certain place or at the same time as another event, we'll associate the two even if they weren't connected. That's why irrational panic attacks occur. For instance, if you have appendicitis after eating celery, you may avoid celery. If you had a wreck on a bridge, you may avoid bridges. If you were mugged in an elevator, you may avoid elevators.

Then we may be terrified about something that's not real. A rope on a dark night may cause the exact same physical trauma as a rattlesnake if you believe it is one. You may have the same reactions to a shadow or a scary movie as you would to an actual attack from a mugger.

Then you may be angry at a supposed snub or a slight before you find out that there were extenuating circumstances. Maybe the person who pushed you was blind. Maybe the person who grabbed your cap was a two-year-old. Maybe you felt real pity and sympathy for a poor beggar until you discovered he's a scam artist in disguise. That's why you can't always trust your feelings.

Solomon knew we often reacted too quickly. He said, "One who is quick-tempered acts foolishly" (Prov 14:17).

Truth

A man standing in front of a bank with a bag was asked, "What are you doing?"

"Waiting for a cab," he answered.

Well, he was, but he'd also just robbed the bank. In this case, the fact was correct, but it didn't express the "truth" because it missed the essential point of the question.

Once, a little boy was asked, "What does your father do?"

He answered, "He shaves every morning."

Again, the fact was correct, but it didn't express the "truth" because it missed the essential point of the question. Truth must include more than a list of correct facts.

The psalmist said, "[God desires] truth in the inward being" (Ps 51:6).

Truth and Faith Containers

"You will know the truth, and the truth will make you free" (John 8:32).

Each scientific fact, biological law, spiritual insight, and technical subject is a piece of a giant jigsaw puzzle. Every piece must interlock with every other piece to form the complete picture, which comprises truth.

If a circle of people stood around the Statue of Liberty, not one of them could ever see the whole, but if each described his view and shared it, then all could know more about the whole. Life experiences give a different view to each person. None are wrong, but none are completely right either. Only if each individual accurately perceives his particular aspect and shares it will the whole be grasped. Of course you won't see it like I do. You can't! You aren't standing where I am. Instead, it's your job to "see it like you do" and to reflect that facet honestly.

The search for truth is different for everyone. People are like potted plants. Each of us has a "faith container." The size of that container isn't important for those limited ones whose roots never touch the sides. However, the size is crucial for those creative ones with a lot of developmental potential. In other words, planting an herb in a cup is okay, but planting an acorn in a cup is asking for trouble!

If a person's belief system isn't large enough and flexible enough to allow for continual growth, one of two things will happen: If the container is weak and shoddy, it will crack under the strain. When such a shattered faith container has to be discarded, the result is usually atheism and cynicism.

If, on the other hand, the faith container is strong and rigid, that will force the intellectual roots to be twisted into grotesque distortions! In the final analysis, small, rigid faith containers stunt growth, stifle productivity, and cause perversions.

We must be able to grow and reach our true potential. The truth will make us free!

Uh-oh and Aha

How do we make progress? How does civilization make progress? Do we steadily grow on a day-to-day basis? Do we have regular goals laid out that we meet year after year? Do we take a certain number of steps or learn a certain number of facts each week?

No! That's not how progress is made. Instead, both individuals and cultures tend to stagnate at a comfort level. As long as things are okay, we quietly exist. Then, all at once, something traumatic happens. We make a mistake! We get into trouble! There's chaos! There's dissonance.! We're hurting, so we stop and say, "Uh-oh!" That's the first point of change.

Then we analyze the situation to see what went wrong. We try to find out what we need to do to get comfortable again. After questioning and analyzing we often discover a new idea or learn a new principle or create a new solution. We see things clearly from a new perspective. So we understand and say, "Aha!" That's the second point of change.

Then we incorporate these new insights into our guidelines for living. That's the third point of change. And that's how we grow and make progress.

Unfortunately, it's usually our problems and tragedies that motivate us. The psalmist said, "It is good for me that I was humbled, so that I might learn your statutes" (Ps 119:71).

Weeds or Wheat

Too many of us see an evil and immediately begin to attack it. That sounds so reasonable, but it's remarkably ineffective. First, a direct attack usually strengthens the very thing we're trying to destroy. For instance, when a nation is attacked, it immediately unifies, marshals its forces, and becomes more powerful than ever.

Furthermore, a direct attack often harms and damages many other things that are positive and good. For instance, you can certainly kill termites by burning down a house, but you ruin a useful structure in the process.

Also, a direct attack often depletes our resources so that we have no time or energy left to accomplish other productive and worthwhile projects. If an organization spends millions on an anti-pornography campaign, there may be nothing left to educate or promote moral responsibility.

When you see evil, don't attack and give it notoriety and strength. Don't attack and risk of hurting good things in the process. Don't attack and get distracted from positive projects. Instead, starve it! If you refuse to feed it, the good will overcome the bad. Jesus once addressed this very issue (see Matt 13:24–30).

As human beings we don't always know the difference between wheat and weeds. That's why we must not make such judgment calls. If we had lived in the first century, most of us would have observed the prostitute, Mary Magdalene, who had seven devils, and said, "There's a weed." And we'd have observed the self-righteous Pharisee, who carefully worshiped and tithed, and said, "There's a wheat plant." But we'd have been dead wrong.

Since we don't know all the causes and motives and consequences of human behaviors, our best course of action is to concentrate on the good and starve the evil.

What Criteria?

What criteria is used to determine which subjects will be preached, taught, and written about? Is it what's needed or what's easy?

Unfortunately, the emphasis is usually on what's easy, what's popular, and what will attract the most people and get the most dollars. Think for a moment. Which of these topics would help more people live good lives: "Considering the mark of the beast?" or "Developing positive relationships in the family?" Yet which topic will draw bigger crowds? Which topic will sell more books?

If an organization announces a meeting with a dramatic, mysterious theme, people come. Yet discussing prophecies and anti-Christs does nothing to prevent drug addictions, street violence, child abuse, divorce, and crime. Learning a few simple principles on how to improve communication or how to handle anger would be much more beneficial.

Why do we gravitate to the paranormal that we might possibly encounter someday when the plain old normal problems of life surround us and overwhelm us every day?

Jesus avoided people who wanted to see signs and wonders, saying, "An evil… generation asks for a sign, but no sign will be given to it" (Matt 12:39).

What Is "Good Enough"?

There are no upper limits on happiness. Things can always be a little bit better. There are no lower limits on misery. Things can always be a little bit worse. So when are things "good enough"?

Unfortunately, as human beings we don't seem capable of finding the optimum point of satisfaction. Instead, we keep pushing until we hit the wall or until circumstances force us to stop. Then the pendulum usually swings to the other extreme. This happens to individuals and groups and entire cultures. Prices are raised until customers refuse to pay. Then there's a recession. Wages spiral upward until businesses go bankrupt. Then everyone loses.

Underprivileged groups want more freedom and more resources, so they push until others become resentful. Then there's backlash. Liberal politicians become more and more liberal until extremes cause conservatives to take over, and then they make the same mistake by becoming more and more conservative until the pattern is reversed.

Why can't we find the balance, the marvelous middle, the optimum point of satisfaction and productivity? Wild, erratic swings between the extremes are nonproductive. Damage is done at both walls.

Paul said he had learned "to be content" (Phil 4:11).

When You See Hoofprints

Not every light in the sky is a UFO! Not every white shape in a cemetery is a ghost! Not every unexplained phenomenon is a supernatural miracle!

Reasonable people always look first for the common, obvious explanation rather than the sensational, mystical explanation.

Many people are so desperate for a little excitement that they hype up every event. That's why *Star Trek* and *The Twilight Zone* were such popular shows. That's why science-fiction paperbacks are such bestsellers. That's why outlandish supermarket tabloids are so prolific.

Yes, we all want meaning and challenge, but life itself is enough of a miracle. We don't need to manufacture manias, fads, and crazes.

The next time you see hoofprints, think horses, not unicorns!

Jesus warned us about deceitful signs, saying, "False messiahs and false prophets will appear and produce sign and wonders, to lead astray, if possible, the elect" (Mark 13:22).

Who Has a Right to an Opinion?

We say, "Everybody has a right to his opinion." Well, maybe they have a right to hold it, but do they have a right to express it? That's the question.

"Free speech" is a precious privilege and a basic democratic principle. Nevertheless, that doesn't mean people are free to slander, to incite a riot, or to shout "Fire!" in a crowded theater. Since words have consequences, people must earn the right to express an opinion.

In wartime we had a motto: "Loose lips sink ships." Likewise, irresponsible, thoughtless, negative statements are destructive. Every time an issue arises, countless individuals without any background knowledge or deep reflection or personal experience immediately begin to make absolute pronouncements.

In fact, when it comes to voicing opinions, everybody is not equal. A person who has lived through a particular tragedy is much more qualified to discuss it than a spectator who has only looked on from a safe distance. A person who has done his homework on a subject through years of research is much more qualified to discuss it than the illiterate whose only information comes from hearsay and Facebook. A person who has paid his dues by hard work, service, and actual involvement in a cause is much more qualified to discuss it than a lazy loafer who has only seen a movie about it. "Shooting from the hip" and reacting before you know the facts are dangerous practices.

Responses to public opinion polls are often ridiculous. A pollster asked a church congregation, "Do you believe the twenty-fifth chapter of Luke is inspired?" Almost all the church members answered, "Yes!" Of course, there is no twenty-fifth chapter of Luke.

A politician asked, "Do you think males and females should matriculate together and use the same curriculum?" Many citizens expressed dismay at the laxity of morals in our universities.

Such anecdotes would be hilarious if they weren't so frightening. When we realize that these same people can elect our leaders and determine our future, we must fear for democracy.

It's better to have no opinion at all than to have a fallacious opinion. Before we sound off, we should ask ourselves these questions: Do I have any experience in this area? Have I studied this issue? Have I invested time and energy in this project?

If we can't answer "yes," maybe we'd better keep our mouths shut! Saying "I don't know enough about that to have an opinion" is a mark of intelligence.

If you must decide something with insufficient information, remain flexible. Once we've voiced an opinion, it becomes harder to change later. Once we've made an adamant statement, it becomes harder to back down. It's better to wait and see than to have to defend foolish positions.

Yes, speech may be free, but we must earn the right to have a responsible opinion.

Solomon said, "If one gives answer before hearing, it is folly and shame" (Prov 18:13).

Why Are We Like That?

Why do some people help while others harm? Why are some people productive while others are nonproductive? Are people born either good or bad? Are people naturally selfish or unselfish?

Everyone is selfish. Every healthy person does what he feels is best for his own personal welfare. It's just that some people have learned to get their satisfaction and pleasure from constructive actions while other have learned to get their satisfaction and pleasure from destructive actions.

For example, if I get my kicks from accomplishing tasks and receiving appreciative responses, then I'll probably be productive and constructive. I'll be that way not because I'm innately better than other people but because I've learned that's the way to secure the rewards I want.

If, on the other hand, I get my kicks from bullying opponents and gaining personal power, then I'll probably be unproductive and destructive. I'll be that way not because I'm innately worse than other people but because I've learned that's the way to secure the rewards I want.

We don't become helpful and productive simply by trying to be nice. That won't work. We become helpful and constructive by changing our definition of satisfaction and pleasure. The bottom line of ethics is this: "Our desired rewards determine our behavior!" If the rewards we desire are positive, our behavior will be positive. If the rewards we desire are negative, our behavior will be negative.

But remember, the psalmist said God will "repay to all according to their work" (Ps 62:12).

Why Do Smart People Do Dumb Things?

Hundreds of normal, educated individuals followed Jim Jones to Guyana and drank cyanide-laced Kool-Aid. Thousands of healthy young men and women join terrorist groups, strap on a bomb, and blow themselves to smithereens. Senior citizens sometimes give their life savings to cult leaders or scam artists. Then we ask ourselves, "Why do smart people do such dumb things?"

Well, it takes intense conditioning and a lot of propaganda to destroy our natural self-preservation instincts and our common sense. The things that can make us become fanatics who are willing to follow manipulative gurus are fear, hatred, and a desperate need for approval, power, or purpose.

To influence and brainwash people, propaganda must do three things: First, it must appeal to emotions, not logic. It must tell followers what they want to hear and express the feelings they aren't able to verbalize. Hitler said, "Aim at emotions and only a limited degree to the intellect."

Next, propaganda must be simplistic and repetitious. People think in concrete images, not in abstract concepts. Visual images and catchy slogans can be effective. Hitler said, "If something is said often enough, it will be believed."

Finally, propaganda must be one-sided, with no opportunity for rebuttal or discussion. In fact, any opposition must be completely discredited and demolished. Propaganda never tries to discover or communicate truth. Instead, it tries to create dangerous polarization and attract gullible followers.

Don't be fooled! Jesus said, "Beware of false prophets, who come to you in sheep's clothing but inwardly are ravenous wolves. You will know them by their fruits" (Matt. 7:15–16).

You Can't Have Just One Piece

A baby reaches for a red bead on his mother's neck and finds that it's stuck to a chain. A Boy Scout grabs a small cord above his cot, and the tent collapses. A puppy pulls a loose thread on a blanket and unravels the entire thing.

These small examples prove an important principle: In life we can't always have one desired item. Instead, we usually find that what we want is part of a whole ball of wax.

You can't buy one side of an old record album to get the song you want. You have to take the flip side too, even if you hate every tune on it.

We can't get an isolated piece of something without inheriting all the causes and consequences and effects that are attached to it.

Unfortunately, most of us don't realize the complexities and interconnectedness of situations and events. In an old story, a couple acquired a magical monkey's paw that would grant the proverbial three wishes. Foolishly, they ask for $10,000 without understanding that money doesn't materialize out of thin air. In a few hours they are informed that their only son has been killed in a horrible accident. As a result they will receive his $10,000 life insurance.

Devastated by grief, they use their second wish to bring him back to life. At midnight a deformed, brain-damaged corpse beats on their door. Terrified, they don't know what to do. Having their son back in that condition is worse than having him dead, so in a final desperate act they use their third wish to undo the havoc they have wrought by their first two wishes.

Life is like that. In ignorance we often pray for a special piece of the universe. But life moves together as an entity. Everything is linked. To have one plea granted we must set up the chain of circumstances necessary to accomplish it, and then we must be willing to reap the inevitable fallout.

Most of us aren't smart enough to comprehend the enormous implications of our requests. In our selfish preoccupation with our own immediate problems, we often overlook the big picture. This is the point God was making in his dramatic confrontation with Job (see Job 38:1, 4–6, 18).

9 781635 282085